AB
TIM

ABOUT TIME

Surviving Ireland's Death Row

PETER PRINGLE

First published 2012

The History Press Ireland
50 City Quay
Dublin 2
www.thehistorypress.ie

British Library Cataloguing in Publication Data.
A catalogue record for this book is available from the British Library.

ISBN 978 1 84588 760 5

Typesetting and origination by The History Press

I dedicate this book to my children and grandchildren
– and to set the record straight

Acknowledgements

This book comes out of my desire to tell my story. I struggled to prove my innocence and I regained my freedom with the help of a great Human Rights lawyer, Greg O'Neill. I remain very grateful to him and to all my friends and family who stood by me. Thanks to Lorna Siggins for her article in *The Irish Times*; to Ronan Colgan of The History Press for expediting the publishing process; to Aonghus and Beth for their valuable and painless editorial assistance; to the legal department for their in-depth examination and advice.

My thanks to Sunny for her support and love.

Prologue

Death cell, Portlaoise Prison, December 1980

'I hear that at least two of us will have to help at his hanging.'

'I heard that too, wonder will they ask for volunteers or will we be ordered to do the job?'

'Either way we would have to be paid extra wages or a bonus.'

'That's right, they'd have to make it worth our while.'

'What would we have to do?'

'When he drops through the trap door of the gallows we'd be underneath ready to pull on his legs to make sure his neck is broken.'

'There'd have to be one for each leg.'

This discussion by three jailers was conducted in my sight and hearing as if I did not exist. 'Happy Christmas, Peter,' I whisper softly as I try to distance myself from the reality of being in the death cell.

I was born in Dublin in 1938. During the war, when I was about 4 years old, I would watch the searchlights in the sky at night and it was very exciting. They were operated from the army barracks at Portobello, nearly a mile away from our house. My pal Nancy, who lived next door, was the same age and we decided that we wanted to see the searchlights up close. So that night, after we were put to bed, we each climbed out of the window and down the drainpipe and headed off, hand-in-hand, to find the barracks. We got into the barracks area through St Mary's College grounds, which were adjacent to the barracks, and hid in some bushes to watch the searchlights. We fell asleep there and were found by the sentries who brought us to the canteen where they gave us cocoa and biscuits.

Meanwhile, our parents had discovered that we were missing and had frantically organised a search. They and the army notified the police and we were soon returned home safe and sound. I couldn't see what the fuss was about. Our parents were so relieved to have us home safe and sound we were not punished – but they checked on us more often when were were put to bed.

My older sister Pauline always looked out for me and my younger brother Pat, especially if some other kid tried to bully either of us. I, in turn, looked out for Pat. That's how it was with brothers and sisters, and not just our family. We built a hut made from scraps of timber in the middle of the bushes. In the autumn when apples were ripe we would go on an expedition to 'box the fox', which is what raiding an orchard to steal apples was called, although we did not think of it as stealing. Sometimes we would be chased by an irate house owner and have to run hell for leather to get away. When we got back to our hideout we would feast on the apples, sharing them with the other youngsters.

If we had difficulty with doing our school homework Dad would look at the problem. He would not solve it for us but would show us the method for solving it and leave us to sort it out ourselves. Then he would look at our result and question us as to how we had resolved it. At the time, I did not really appreciate his wisdom.

My Dad rented a bog on the Featherbeds, an area of the Dublin Mountains to the south of the city. He would go up there on Saturdays and Sundays and cut the turf. Sometimes he'd bring me with him, on the crossbar of his bicycle as far as Rathfarnham, where we would board a big turf lorry, bike and all, and be driven the rest of the way up to the Featherbeds. While Dad was cutting turf my job was 'footing the turf', stacking it in a special way so that the wind would dry it out. We would light a fire and boil tea and eat our sandwiches for lunch. I loved being in the mountains. Come evening time, we would travel home by bike as it was all downhill. We seemed to whizz along the road and be home in no time. When the turf was all cut and dried and ready to be taken home, the turf lorry would collect it and bring it to our house and tip it in the back lane. Our neighbours and all the kids on the street would help to bring it into our back yard where my Dad would stack it properly. Then there'd be a big party, with Guinness and food for the men and lemonade and cakes for the kids – and pennies too.

My grandfather lived in County Kildare, near Rathangan. He was originally from Dublin, but left the city when they started building outside of the two canals. He reckoned the city was getting too big. He and my grandmother had a small farm and every summer I looked forward to going to them on holidays. It was magical for me, being in the country and enjoying their country ways. They had two cows, a pony, pigs, hens, geese and ducks. There were fields and woods to roam, and a river at the bottom of the big field. Grandmother made homemade bread, cakes and butter. And in the evenings around the fireplace, it was so warm and snug. Listening to the stories and local news I got ever more drowsy. I would then be carried down to the room and into bed, to dreams wrapped in eiderdown quilt and not stirring until daylight. Sometimes I would lie in bed and listen to the chug, chug, chug of the barges as they passed along the canal about a mile away. The sound of the barge got louder on the night air as it came closer, and then it would fade away into the distance. And I would dream of its journey and of travelling on it.

Sometimes my grandparents told stories about the Fairies. And they believed in their existence too. Each night before retiring, Grandmother put a glass of milk and a plate of cake or scones in the window for the Fairies. And it was always empty in the morning. I remember one time walking in the woods with Grandad, and we came on a fox's covert. He pointed it out to me and told me that this particular opening was also the entrance to the Fairy world under the ground. The Fairies, or 'Little People' as they sometimes called them, lived underground and in the hillside and one must always respect them. This was wise, as the Little People could be lethal if they were upset or treated with disrespect. Grandad told me to keep the memories and not lose sight of the important things handed down to us through the generations.

I remember one time Aunt Mainie, who lived with my grand-parents, had to visit the dentist in Kildare Town, which was several miles away. The evening before, Grandad brushed down the pony, polished the harness, and shined the buckles and the brass rails on the trap in preparation for the journey. We were up early for breakfast, and then I went with Grandad to get the pony ready for the trip. When he had been harnessed to the trap I held him while Grandad went to put on his Sunday suit. Grandmother and Aunt Mainie were all dressed up too, hats and gloves and all. The trap was a two-wheeled light cart entered through a door at the back. Seating was along each side, passengers facing inwards. Grandad sat to the front on the outside and I sat opposite him. Grandmother and Aunt Mainie sat to the back and away we went, Grandad gently clucking to the pony to start him trotting. After a few miles, when the pony had settled in to his task, Grandad passed the reins to me while he filled his pipe and lit up. Satisfied that I was doing alright, he settled back and enjoyed his smoke while I tried to appear casual driving along, especially if we met anyone on the road. It was the most exciting event of my life up to then.

In Kildare we watered the pony at the horse trough in the square. Then Grandad tied him to a tree and put a nose bag of oats around his neck and the pony munched contentedly. Grandmother had gone with Mainie to the dentist, and I strolled about the town with Grandad. He met lots of men he knew and I was introduced to them. Two of them even slipped me a sixpenny piece with a wink. After the dentist we all went to the hotel for lunch but Aunt Mainie was only able to sip a bowl of soup.

I don't remember much about the trip home. With all the excitement of the day, the motion of the trap and the rhythm of the pony's hooves, I fell asleep and only woke up as we were turning into the farmyard. But I helped Grandad un-harness the pony and wipe him down and stow the harness before going up to the house for supper. I don't remember going to bed either, but I slept the night through. The summers passed quickly. Then it was back to school.

About 1946 there was a teachers' strike, and my pals and I thought we would be off school and have great fun. But my parents had other ideas for me, to my great disappointment. The strike was by lay teachers, which meant the Christian Brothers schools remained open, so my parents enrolled me in St Laurence O'Toole's in Seville Place on the opposite side of the city. On my first day, my Mum took me on the bus to show me the way and collected me after school. That evening I was asked if I could make the journey on my own. I said that I could, because I thought this was expected of me. Although I was afraid, I kept my fear to myself. No doubt if I had spoken up my Mum or Dad would have escorted me, or sought a different school for me.

Thereafter, I would walk to Kelly's Corner and take the number 20 bus right across the city. I used to sit upstairs, in the front seat if possible, feeling much older than my 7 years. Walking down Seville Place to the school from the bus, I had to go under a long railway bridge with separate arches for traffic and pedestrians. It was half-dark and I was in strange territory. I braced myself, worked up the courage and ran as fast as I could through the long archway as though my life depended on it! On my second day at school the class bully picked on me and I had to fight him at lunchtime behind the bicycle shed in the yard. The other kids gathered around and I knew that I must not show my fear. In desperation, I fought like mad and to my surprise the bully gave up quickly. After that, I was accepted by the other kids and my time was happy enough at that school. I was big for my age and quickly learned not to back down. Most times I didn't have to fight. I was glad of that as I never liked fighting.

At that time, there was a lot of horse-drawn traffic in Dublin. The Post Office main sorting depot was in Amiens Street, which was on my route home from school. Instead of taking the bus I'd walk to the sorting depot, and when one of the post wagons, loaded with mail bags and drawn by two horses, trotted out from the depot heading across town I would 'scut' on the back of it and get a free ride across the city. Sometimes, someone would yell, 'Scut behind! Lash the whip!' and the driver sitting high in his box at the front would crack his long whip behind him to scare me off the back of his wagon. As soon as I heard the yell I would crouch down as low as possible, only straightening up again after hearing its 'crack' above my head. It was exciting, and I loved it. And I managed to save my bus fare to buy toffees, and sometimes cigarettes. I was rapidly becoming streetwise and learning to take care of myself.

When the teachers' strike ended my parents got me into Synge Street Christian Brothers School, which was within walking distance from home. I enjoyed the junior classes, but as I advanced through the primary school I had some nasty experiences with Brothers who seemed to enjoy punishing us. At the time, corporal punishment was accepted in schools. One Brother had coins stitched inside his leather strap and being slapped by him was tough. Sometimes he would take a boy by the ear from his desk to the front of the class, grab the short hairs above the ears and lift him off the ground by the hair. When he did it to me it was hard not to scream or cry. But when I saw that that was what he wanted I gritted my teeth and tried to stay silent, no matter what pain he would inflict on me.

The Brothers were not the only hazard in that school. The boys tended to pal together in groups, or gangs, for self-preservation. The rivalry between groups was mostly friendly, but occasionally there would be a fight. On one occasion I was picked on by a boy called Mac from another group. I had no option but to fight him. We were caught and punished by one of the Brothers, who gave us an extra leathering because neither of us would blame the other. No matter our differences, we had to stand together when faced by a brutal Brother. We became friends thereafter, and I had no more trouble.

Some days I would skip school, happily wandering the streets or through the park at St Stephen's Green. This was called 'mitching'. But when I returned to school I'd be behind the rest of the class in my studies, which brought even more trouble from the sadistic Brothers. Ultimately I decided it was better to attend and try to stay unnoticed, rather than give them an excuse to focus on me.

Our dog Spot was a floppy-eared mongrel, black with a white spot on his chest. He'd follow me most of the way to school and meet me on my way home. When I crossed Richmond Street he would usually turn back. But one morning he came after me and was knocked down by an army truck. I ran back to him and held him in my arms, crying my heart out. Soldiers got down from the back of the truck laughing, and I became fierce angry. I brought Spot to the veterinary hospital across from where the accident happened. But the poor thing was too badly injured and had to be put down. I was devastated.

I became an altar boy in our local church in Rathmines. There was a priest there who was shell-shocked from the war and who was eccentric, especially in his speech. His voice could range from a quiet whisper to a loud shout almost in the same sentence – and he did not seem to be aware of this. The other mass servers were scared of him. But I liked him, and was chosen to serve him at mass a couple of times each week. He was always allocated to say his mass at a side alter, and when very few people were in church. This often meant that I'd be a half hour late getting to school, which the Brothers forgave because I was serving at mass. The priest sometimes gave me a shilling after mass and that was a mighty bonus as far as I was concerned, considering that I could get in to the cinema for six pence and the Saturday matinée for four pence.

'Any oul rags, bottles, or bones? Any oul rags, bottles or bones?' called out the ragman as he came into our street with his horse and cart.

We loved seeing him come, and we would run to our houses to see if we could get anything for him. 'Mum! Have we any old rags for the ragman?'

'Get out of that and don't be annoying me, there's nothing for that old fella unless I give him the rags off my own back! Go on out to play!' But we would search in the garden shed and maybe find a few empty bottles and the ragman would pay us with a toffee apple or maybe a windmill. This was a sort of windmill on a stick, which rotated if we ran along holding it up to the wind.

We would not give him jam jars because they were too valuable to us then. Glass was scarce due to the war, and we could get into the Saturday matinée at the local cinema for two pence and two large jam jars. Without our jam jars it cost four pence to get in. We had two cinemas near us on Rathmines Road, the Stella and the Princess.

The latter was commonly known as 'the Prinner' and was the only cinema locally to accept jam jars in part payment for entry to the matinée on Saturday. The queue outside the Prinner was always long – a crowd of laughing, talking, yelling youngsters holding tight to their jam jars. Johnny, the usher, was a tough little Dubliner who could control any mob of chisellers. When the concertina gates were opened, Johnny appeared in his tacky maroon uniform and stood at the head of the queue, hands on hips, and let out a roar. 'Quiet!'

There was instant silence. He proceeded along the queue, carrying a large basket. And as a kid placed his jam jars into the basket, Johnny handed a chit to the kid in exchange. When all the jam jars were exchanged for chits and he had deposited the basket inside, Johnny would allow us into the cinema. Once inside, there would be a mad rush to get seats. Everyone wanted to get up on to the balcony, and that's where the first of the queue went. If we did not make the balcony we made sure to be near the back and under the balcony. Nobody wanted to sit downstairs in front of the balcony, because sometimes kids in the front row of the balcony would pee over the front instead of leaving their seats to go to the toilet in case they would either lose their seat or miss an exciting part of the film. Johnny had his work cut out keeping order in the darkness of the cinema, as he ranted up and down the aisles flashing his torch along the rows. We had an economic crisis when glass became plentiful again and the value of the empty jam jars fell, first to one penny for a large jar and ultimately to no value towards entry into the Prinner.

When rationing ended and fruit could be imported again, the excitement of seeing my first bananas and oranges was wonderful. Sometimes, as banana lorries were stopped at traffic lights kids would climb up the back and throw bunches of bananas off to the other kids, who would gather them up. Then at the next corner the bananas would be shared out. We never thought about the dangers involved in such an escapade.

2

Just before I turned 14 I left school and went to work. Actually, I didn't just 'leave' school, I had no other option. One of the Christian Brothers had a boy out in front of the class giving him a beating, while the rest of us sat petrified in fear. To everyone's surprise, and none more than myself, I shouted out, 'Leave him alone!'

The Brother left him alone sure enough, only he called me out instead. I was terrified at what I'd done and knew I was really in for a trouncing. He grabbed me by my sweater and as he drew back his fist to punch me I suddenly realised that I was as big as he was and in desperation lashed out and sent him flying. He stumbled back, more in shock than from my wild punch, and banged into the blackboard, falling over it and bringing it down with him. The class gave a great cheer, a frenzied release of tension. There was a moment when I felt great, as the class continued to cheer and beat on the desktops. The Brother scrambled on the floor trying to get untangled from the blackboard and to his feet. I could see his face bloated red with anger and I knew I had to get out of there. I quickly gathered up my books and headed for the door, with him screaming as he scrambled to his feet, 'Quiet! Quiet! Get back here Pringle!'

I kept going. But with the front door to the street in sight, I was caught by the head Brother. He wanted to know what a boy was doing in the corridor leaving the school during class time. When I told him I was leaving for good he put his arm around my shoulder and walked me to the door saying he was sorry to see me go as he was sure I'd been happy in the school. This puzzled me as it was the first time he'd ever spoken to me and I was always careful to stay well out of his way. As we got to the door he said he wanted to give me good advice as I headed out into the world. He told me to say my prayers and to beware of loose women! And that was it. I was free. I walked away from the school towards home, exhilarated and smiling as I remembered the expression of shock on the face of the Brother as he fell over. But then I thought about facing my parents and that took the smile off my face. I looked in every shop window along the way and stopped to watch a barge go through the canal lock.

When I got home I told my Mum what happened. She said we would wait until Dad came home and let him sort it out. Dad came home and we had dinner, but my stomach was tight as I waited for the inevitable.

'Tom, Peter has something to tell you. Go ahead Peter.'

I then told him what had happened. As his face darkened, I explained how terrible it was at that school and that I was never going back there. He sat a few minutes looking at me and my Mum as he considered the whole thing. Turning to Mum he said, 'Maybe we can sort this out if we go speak to the Brother.' Before they could take that idea any further, I insisted again that, no matter what, I would not return to that school. After more discussion and attempts to change my mind, he finally said, 'Well, if you won't go to school you'll just have to get a job.'

A few days later he spoke to a friend and I started work the following week.

My first job was with a wholesale tobacconist and confectioners in the city centre. I started work at £1 10s per week, gave up £1 to my Mum and had 10 shillings for myself. In a period of unemployment and emigration it was good to have any kind of work. Everyone was friendly and I quickly became used to the job. The mornings were usually spent packing goods on the shelves. Afternoons were hectic as orders came in and had to be prepared for delivery the following morning. In my second week the boss asked me why I did not cycle to work. When I told him I did not own a bike and was saving to buy one, he went in to his office and came out with an order to a bicycle trader. He said I could pick myself a bike and he would deduct the payments from my wages. I bought a bike at trade price and was well pleased with myself. We agreed on 10 shillings a week. The following week when I got my wages there was still £1 10s in the envelope. I went to the boss and asked if he had forgotten to deduct for the bike and he told me he had given me a 10 shilling raise. Cycling to work in the mornings was mostly downhill and I could fly along. Going home in the evenings I had to pedal hard uphill, except when I could catch on to the back of a truck and be pulled along. The excitement of that was greater than any thought of its danger.

When I started work in 1952 there was a lot of poverty in Ireland. I remember seeing the unemployed marching in the streets, demanding work. People were poorly dressed, and poorly paid. The unemployed had barely enough food to feed their families. The pawn shops were thriving businesses, and it was not unusual for the Sunday clothes to be pawned on Monday and redeemed again on Saturday for mass on Sunday. Bellmen, as they were called because their horse had a bell around the neck which rang as it moved, went around with their horse-drawn carts selling coal by the stone (14 lbs) or by the bucket. Very few people could afford to buy a bag of coal. Grocery shops sold loose tea by the ounce, and butter likewise. Beef dripping was sold and spread on bread instead of butter and was often referred to as 'bread and dip' when the dripping was heated on a pan. My Dad used to repair our shoes when the soles and heels wore out, by placing the shoe on a last and fitting new soles and heels by hammering in little nails. Then he trimmed the leather with a knife and dyed the edges. When he had finished, the shoes looked almost new again. Nobody I knew had a telephone or a car. One man on our street had an old motorbike, but otherwise the main means of transport was the bicycle if one was lucky enough to have such a luxury. Going by 'shanks' mare', or walking, was the norm.

After a few months I was able to buy a rucksack and hiking boots and I took up hill walking. This quickly became my favourite way of spending the weekends. I joined the youth hostelling association, hiked to all of the mountain ranges in the country and walked them all. I developed a strong love for the west of Ireland and often headed off from Dublin to climb the Twelve Bens in Connemara.

The following summer, when I was 14, I had my first holiday from work. I wanted to hitch hike to Kerry and west Cork to climb the mountains and visit some historical sites I was interested in seeing. Two of my pals from the neighbourhood, Mike and Seán, agreed to travel with me, and the three of us were to leave on the Saturday. My parents accepted my going away hiking at weekends, but heading off for two weeks caused them serious concern. After long negotiations, however, they agreed to the holiday. But three days before the departure date Mike pulled out and on the Friday evening Seán told me he couldn't go either. I swore each of them to secrecy and on Saturday set off on my own, my parents still believing I was to join up with the two lads down the road.

The first day I hitched to Bansha in County Tipperary. I walked to the hostel at Ballydavid Wood and stayed there that night, and in the morning I walked to Bansha for Mass. The priest gave a long sermon, his theme being 'Do unto others as you would they do to you'. On the walk back to the hostel it began to rain heavily. A car came along and I tried to hitch a lift. It was the priest. Not only did he not stop, but he drove through a pool of water, splashing me. My legs were soaked. I became angry with the priest and his total disregard for what he had just preached, deciding there and then that I was finished with the Catholic Church, God and all that nonsense, as I saw it then. That decision seemed to me to be in harmony with my being away on holidays on my own, and I felt good within myself.

Back at the hostel I changed clothes, collected my rucksack and set off up the slopes of the Galtee Mountains. I walked the mountains all that day, climbing Galtee Mór, the highest point, before heading down the far side to the hostel at Mountain Lodge, where I stayed that night. The next morning I sent my parents a postcard explaining that I was on my own and doing well and asking them not to worry. I went on my way and hitched to Kerry.

I climbed Mangerton and Carrauntoohil, the highest mountain in Ireland. The day was clear and the scenery was magical and I felt like I was achieving something great. I stayed in a hostel near Killarney where I met a girl who wanted to see the Gap of Dunloe, so we hired ponies and rode up to the top of the Gap. She was a nice girl and fun to be with. When we got back down and returned the ponies my behind was very sore. We explored the area together on foot for a couple of days, courting a little but nothing more than that.

Next day, I headed off alone to explore the Beara Peninsula. I had read about O'Sullivan Beara, the seventeenth-century chieftain who had to leave his homelands after the Irish were defeated in the Battle of Kinsale at Christmas 1601. He set out with one thousand of his people – warriors, women and children – to march to Leitrim to join with O'Rourke of Breffny, who was still undefeated. They were harried and attacked all along the way, with less than thirty surviving to reach their destination. I was fascinated by the story and wanted to walk the peninsula where they had lived. It is rugged country and very beautiful. Walking the hills with the Atlantic to the north and to the south was a great experience for me, and I imagined how it must have been back then when it was covered in forests.

Heading north, I made a stop at Foulksrath Castle, County Kilkenny, which was also a hostel. I had heard that this sixteenth-century Norman castle was haunted and so wanted to experience staying there. By this time I had very little money left, so as opportunity arose I gathered a few potatoes and carrots from a garden as I passed by and cooked them for my dinner in the hostel later that evening.

There were four other young men staying in the hostel that night. The men's dormitory was two floors up a winding stone stairway, with the women's another floor above. As we were in our dormitory getting ready for bed one young man went back downstairs for something. On his return he told us that he had met a beautiful young woman coming upstairs as he was descending. She had long fair hair, wore a long white nightdress and held a candle to light her way. As he stepped aside to let her pass she smiled as she continued upwards. We assumed she, and perhaps some friends, had been late arrivals, which explained why we had not seen her earlier. The following morning at breakfast, the lad who had seen her told the old woman who ran the hostel. Smiling quietly, she said, 'That was herself, she is here all the time', as if it was nothing unusual. Later she explained that 'herself' was the ghost of the castle. I stayed a second night in the hope that I might meet her, but she did not show herself to me.

I was nervous as I approached the house on my return from the two-week break. I accepted that I was wrong to have gone off as I did but knew also that I had to do it. My folks gave out to me, of course, but were glad I was home safe. They had finally come to accept that I could look after myself, and I think they were actually a little proud of that. I resumed work on Monday and life returned to normal, although my friendship with Mike and Seán was changed and I did not hike with either of them again.

When I could afford it I would take the boat to Holyhead, leaving on Friday evening directly from work, to spend the weekend on the Welsh mountains. I bought most of my hiking gear in Wales as prices were much lower than in Ireland. I'd arrive back in Dublin in time for work on Monday morning. Scotland was also a favourite place but on my money I got there much less frequently than to Wales.

As I gained more experience and better equipment I either slept out or in huts I had located in the forests. Sometimes I walked with a friend, but quite often I went alone. I liked being on my own in the mountain vastness and enjoyed the sense of self-sufficiency.

Around this time I was initiated to full sex by an older woman whose husband was working in England. At my Mum's suggestion I used to do errands for the woman on occasion. One day, when I brought her groceries from the shop, she answered the door in a dressing gown. And when I had put the box of groceries on her kitchen table she put her arms around me and kissed me. Before I knew it she was leading me to her bedroom. Then she was naked and undressing me, caressing and fondling me. And I was touching her. Soon we were on her bed and she showed me how to make love. At first I was frightened and really did not know what to do, but she soothed and guided me. And it was wonderful. She was sweet, kind and fun. It was like a whole new world had been opened to me. I was sure I was in love with her. She swore me to secrecy, otherwise she would never be with me again. Actually, we were only together on three other occasions over the next few weeks, as her husband came home soon after and they went to live in England. When she left I missed her, and was broken-hearted for a while. I had girlfriends from time to time, and liked being with girls. But I found that being with women a little older was better, especially sex-wise.

At work I did odd jobs as well as helping make up the orders for the van to deliver. Sometimes I would go with the van as helper and for me that was the best part of the job. Dermot the driver was quite a character and I loved being on the rounds with him. He had a caustic Dublin wit and cynicism, never short of a comment or retort no matter the occasion. Each day after his lunch Dermot would take a nap on a chaise longue in his kitchen. 'That's what the aristocrats do for their digestion and if they can do it so can I!' Dermot taught me how to drive. At lunchtime he used to drop me home before heading to his own place. But one day he went via his house and got out of the van, telling me to drive myself home and pick him up an hour later. That was how I started to drive regularly. I was 16 and eligible for a driving licence, which I got later.

One afternoon on our rounds we went into Tommy Ryan's pub on Haddington Road so Dermot could listen to a horse race on the radio. He had a pint and I had an orange. A tall man swept in dramatically, called for a pint and pulled a stool into the middle of the room, greeting everyone in a loud voice. He had on a gabardine coat and wide-brimmed hat. He knew Dermot and asked, 'Who's your young friend?' introducing himself as 'Paddy'. He went on to regale the company with stories and jokes and had everyone laughing, including the publican. When we left, Dermot told me that was Paddy Kavanagh, the poet. When I made a comment about his unusual behaviour he said, 'Ah, you don't understand. He's a poet.' He went on to explain that Paddy was most likely broke and by entertaining the company he ensured a flow of porter. I was surprised at the respect and even love shown to Paddy by everyone in the pub, and only later understood Dermot's comment about being a poet. To be a poet in Ireland engendered respect, awe and allowance for eccentricity. Poets have always been very important to the Irish psyche throughout our history.

History was very interesting for me. I was an avid reader and the library and second-hand bookshops were my source, as well as my Aunt Molly. A real rebel, she lived her life according to her own dictates, having run away from home to join a travelling show to be with her lover. Whenever she was in Dublin she visited us, bringing me books by such writers as Nabokov, Dickens, Tolstoy, Faulkner, Steinbeck and Hardy. We would then discuss those books on her next visit. I read anything I could about Irish history and learned something about the 1916 Rising and the struggle for independence. Of the 1916 leaders, James Connolly and Thomas Clarke made the biggest impression on me. I was inspired by

Connolly for having organised the Citizen Army for the defence of the working class, and Clarke for his dedicated perseverance in the struggle. I admired people like Tom Barry, Ernie O'Malley, Peadar O'Donnell and Michael Collins for their parts in the War of Independence. The Civil War grieved me but my sympathies were with the republicans. I respected the men who went to Spain to fight fascism and had no time at all for those who went to support Franco. Nor had I any time for the Blueshirts, as the Irish fascist organisation was called.

Because of my interest in politics I was excited when Jack Murphy, a candidate for the unemployed, was elected to the Dáil (the Irish parliament). This was a cause of great hope for the unemployed and poor of Dublin. But as he was a lone voice in the Dáil, without backing or support or political experience, he seldom got a hearing. Rumours were spread that he was a communist and he became a subject of scorn in the media. As a result he locked himself in a room in a terraced house near Christchurch Cathedral and went on hunger strike to draw attention to the injustice and inequity of the political system. Again, the black propaganda got to work, this time alleging that he was secretly having food delivered to him and that his hunger strike was a sham. Ultimately he came off the hunger strike, resigned his Dáil seat and emigrated with his family to Canada. This brought an end to the Unemployed Workers Movement. It was reckoned on the streets that the Archbishop of Dublin had influenced Jack to give up his struggle and leave the country. It was even said that the church paid the fare to Canada and arranged for employment and accommodation for Jack and his family.

It disturbed me that Ireland was in such a mess of poverty, unemployment, and emigration and that the existing system seemed unable to make things any better. The fact that the country was divided and partly occupied by Britain influenced my thinking strongly. But what could I do about it? Then one evening I saw a man selling the United Irishman paper outside the General Post Office in O'Connell Street. I bought a copy and learned that Sinn Féin still existed. I read the reports of IRA arms raids on British Army barracks in Armagh and Omagh in the North, and found it very interesting and exciting that there was still some resistance to British rule in Ireland. Shortly thereafter I located the George Plant Cumann of Sinn Féin in Crumlin and became a member. I was 16 years old.

The main activities in the branch were attending meetings and selling the monthly publication, the United Irishman. But these activities were too mundane for me. What I really wanted was to make contact with the IRA. Britain still occupied part of my country and the only people I could see who might do something about it were republicans, and that meant the IRA. It seemed logical to me that territorial independence was essential if we were ever to have economic independence. Two IRA prisoners in Belfast, Tom Mitchell and Philip Clarke, were elected MPs in Mid-Ulster and Fermanagh/South Tyrone constituencies in the 1955 elections with a total of over 150,000 votes. This indicated strong support for republicanism.

A year later I joined the IRA. Contrary to popular belief, it was not easy to locate or join. In fact, it was far easier to get out than to get in. For its own survival, the IRA had to check out each new recruit. The fact that my Dad was a Garda, as police officers are called in Ireland, was not an obstacle to my being accepted into the organisation, and neither did it deter me from entering. I knew that I was embarking on a road very different to the one he was travelling, but I felt I was correct and that was sufficient for me. There was a three-month course for recruits. This induction or education course included history, politics, IRA rules and regulations, debate and question-and-answer sessions, all aimed at the recruiting officer being able to decide whether to accept or reject a potential volunteer. We were told in no uncertain terms not to expect anything romantic about being in the IRA, that it was not a democratic organisation. It was the Irish Republican Army and required discipline and obedience from its volunteers. It was made clear to us that we might have to face the prospect of imprisonment, injury or even death. If we were not prepared for such possibilities, we were told, we should withdraw and could do so at any time. There was one condition on leaving: no talking to anybody about the organisation afterwards.

I did not tell my family or anyone else that I had joined the IRA. And my already established practice of hill walking at weekends was a perfect cover for weekends spent training in the mountains. This involved learning the use of explosives, firearms training and field craft. I already knew how to read maps, use a compass and live in the hills, which was an advantage. There were also meetings during the week called parades, where we were instructed in the use of small arms, tactics and theory.

The IRA was working towards starting an armed campaign against the British occupation of the six counties in the North. The aim of the campaign was basically to break down the British-controlled administration in the occupied territory and force the withdrawal of Crown forces. It had been successful in training men to a high standard, but was unable to hold such trained volunteers in check when they wanted action. As a result, there was a split in the Dublin leadership led by Joe Christle, a charismatic and vocal advocate of immediate action. Joe and his followers believed, and not without some credibility, that the leadership of the IRA, being older men, were reluctant to take on British forces in Ireland. The raid on Roslea RUC barracks by Saor Uladh (Free Ulster), a small group led by Liam Kelly, during which Connie Green, a leading member, was killed, also put the IRA leadership under pressure to commence action in the North.

In order to avoid a bigger split, the leadership opted to start the campaign in the winter of 1956. The support for action against the British had not been promoted sufficiently within the civilian population of the North or South, however, so the decision went in the face of the basic law of guerrilla fighting – it cannot succeed without the support of the civilian population. But at the time I was young and idealistic and such matters did not concern me.

What later became known as the Border Campaign began on 12 December 1956. There were a number of operations, spectacular at the time, which brought support from people and condemnation from church and state. The raid on Brookeborough in County Fermanagh in January 1957, in which two IRA volunteers, Seán South from Limerick and Fergal O'Hanlon from Monaghan, were killed, aroused huge feelings in the country.

In May 1957, while on a weekend training exercise, I was among thirty-eight volunteers who were surrounded and arrested by armed detectives. We were on a night trek along the Glencree Valley in County Wicklow. During the night, I noticed the lights of a lot of traffic on the roads above us on each side of the valley and knew from my hiking experience and my familiarity with the area that this was very unusual. I could tell that there were trucks on the roads. My alarm bells went off as I wondered what trucks might be doing on those quiet roads, all travelling in one direction in the middle of the night. I instinctively felt that we should leave the valley and move up to the high ground above the road. I brought this to the attention of those in command of our column but they chose not to act. When we reached the head of the valley with daylight coming on, we found that we were surrounded by armed detectives. I have no doubt that the traffic I had observed was the Gardaí and that they had been informed about our location that night.

We were taken in custody to the Bridewell, a Garda station and holding centre in Dublin. We were each charged under the Offences Against the State Act, 1939, with 'failing to account for your movements', which is to say refusing to answer interrogations while in Garda custody, a provision that was years later struck down as being unconstitutional. At the time of my arrest, my Dad was still a serving policeman. He was horrified to learn that his 18-year-old son was in the IRA.

During my detention I was taken to an office where I was confronted by my Dad and Detective Superintendent Michael Gill, the head of Special Branch. After a short while Gill offered me a deal, a job in Special Branch if I would give up my involvement in the republican movement. He told me that if I agreed I would be on the payroll immediately, that I did not have to sign anything. He explained that I was going to be sentenced to three months and that if I wanted to I could do the time in Mountjoy without anyone knowing about the deal. My salary would be paid into a bank for me and all I had to do was keep him informed about what was going on in the prison. Then, when I was released, I could resign from the IRA and officially join his staff.

My Dad told me I should accept this 'great offer', and that I could trust Superintendent Gill, to which I replied, 'Like Gantley trusted him?' With that, Gill let out a roar and charged across the room at me. My Dad got between us, which saved me a severe beating at least. I was hustled from the room, my last glimpse being of my Dad holding back Gill who was shouting abuse after me, red-faced and very angry. I was taken back to the cell by a very disturbed Garda, obviously curious and in awe of the superintendent's rage.

The background was that in February 1948 the then head of the Special Branch, Chief Superintendent Gantley, was shot dead leading a party of armed Special Branch on a mission in Dublin. He was found to have been accidentally shot dead by one of his own officers, but there were rumours going around that Gill had played some part in the incident leading to Gantley's death.

Gill was correct and I was sentenced to three months in Mountjoy. Built of grey stone, Mountjoy was a grim Victorian prison, designed like a wheel, four cell wings – A, B, C and D – radiating out from a circle and the fifth leg being administration. Each wing had four floors, called landings. I was to be held in D Wing with the other republican prisoners. The other wings held ordinary prisoners such as thieves, burglars and con men.

We were brought to the prison in closed vans. It felt surreal stepping out of the van within the prison walls. I was trapped, and about to be caged, for the first time in my life. Directed into administration, we were individually processed into the system. I was asked my name, date of birth, address, next of kin, and religion. Then I was taken into the circle where I could see along the length of each wing. The gate into D Wing was opened and I was taken through to the cell allocated to me. The other cells were all locked, but I could hear the hum of voices calling out from behind the solid cell doors, timber on the outside and metal on the inside.

When I was put into the cell, reality quickly set in as the heavy door clanged shut behind me, reverberating through the cell and into my head. Even though I had been warned that I might be locked up, it was a shocking moment for me. I was totally enclosed, on my own, as in a tomb, with the resounding echo of the banging door fading through the stillness.

The cell was about 10 feet by 7. There was a barred window high up on the end wall, and the walls were painted a faded pale green. The door was solid steel with a small round hole, known as the 'Judas hole', about 2 inches in diameter. Outside the hole was a sliding flap, which the jailer slid aside when he looked in to check on me. The cell had an army-type metal bed with a mattress, three grey blankets, two sheets and a pillow. There was a small table, a stool, a locker and that was it. On the table were a tray, two mugs, a knife, a fork and a spoon, all made of aluminium. A heating pipe ran along the length of the prison wing through each cell. If someone banged on it, the sound travelled along the pipe and everyone heard it. There was no toilet or sink and no running water. I was provided with a plastic potty, like a child might use. This was the total sanitation facility in the cell.

I made up the bed and lay on it, wondering how on earth I would be able to cope with being there. I worried about my family, especially my Dad and how he was, given the shock of my being in prison when he was a police officer. On my own behalf I was comforted knowing that my comrades were nearby. Deciding that the best thing to do was try to get some sleep, I got into bed and slept till morning. I was awakened by sounds of the prison stirring, with jailers calling out their count, keys rattling and doors being opened.

When my turn came, I went out onto the landing and met the other men as they left their cells. I learned how to slop out my potty at a toilet at the end of the landing, then we all went on parade and marched to the circle to collect breakfast. In the circle area, a steel triangle hung from the ceiling with a steel baton hanging beside it. When the signal was given to open cells or lock them, and to announce mealtimes, the triangle was beaten, using the steel baton in rotation around its inside. The sound rang through the prison. This was the same triangle that Brendan Behan wrote about in his song 'The Ould Triangle'. And sure enough, it did go 'jingle jangle' when struck by the baton. Funny the things one thinks of when confronted by overwhelming circumstances.

Breakfast consisted of a mug of tea, a small loaf of bread made in the prison, a half mug of milk and a plate of porridge. Back in my cell, I discovered that the bread was like dough, only the crust was edible. The porridge was lumpy and stodgy and inedible. Resigning myself to having just a mug of tea, I lifted the metal mug to my lips only to find that the mug got as hot as the tea, and it was impossible to drink the tea while hot without burning my lips. So much for breakfast!

There was a regimen to prison life. Cell doors were opened about 8.30 a.m. We were locked in our cells for dinner and locked up again at 8.30 p.m. for the night. When we were not confined to our cells we had access to the landing, the recreation cell and the yard – except between 4 p.m. and 5 p.m. when we could not use the yard because that's when the 'screws' (as jailers were called) went for their tea.

Our outdoor exercise was in the prison yard attached to D Wing. There was a wall around the yard with barbed wire on top. We could see the very high outer wall beyond, and there was a wide passageway in between the two walls patrolled by jailers.

We had our own elected authority, an OC (officer commanding) and his staff, and we refused to deal with or acknowledge the prison authorities except through them. We were not criminals. We were political prisoners, more like prisoners of war, and we behaved accordingly. Republican prisoners didn't wear prison clothes or do prison work. Consequently, we didn't get remission on our sentences.

We were allowed visits and letters which meant we were in touch with loved ones and the outside world. We had a radio in the recreation cell and could listen to the news. We had lots of reading material and our morale was high. We could play table tennis on the landing and kicked a football around in the yard. As well as that, we played cards in the recreation cell or even in each other's cell. We also had our own education system of classes in Irish, History, Guerrilla Tactics, and Engineering. We were allowed a bath once a week when we paraded in small groups to the bath house, which was on A Wing. We were allowed food parcels back then, which was just as well, as it would have been difficult if we had to exist on prison food only.

It was during this time that the Catholic hierarchy issued a decree stating that unless a member of the IRA left that organisation, he could not receive the sacraments and would be excommunicated from the church. The opposition of the church to the IRA was very strong, but there were some individual priests who did not agree with that policy. Excommunication was a very serious matter for some of the volunteers and caused them considerable qualms of conscience. Since I had already left the church, it did not bother me.

The Mater Hospital was across the road from the prison. From the top of the steps leading down to the yard we could see the flat roof of the nurses' quarters where they often sunbathed in the afternoons.

Although they were far away, in more ways than one, we could see them and they could see us. And we used to wave to each other holding a bright cloth in our hand and making large letters against the grey background of our building. It was simple fun, which in a few cases developed into friendships.

Before my sentence was up, the state brought in internment for up to five years under the same Offences Against the State Act, 1939. Internment is imprisonment without charge or trial. This new development meant that when our various sentences were finished in Mountjoy we would be transferred to The Curragh Military Camp where the state had established its internment camp. In response to this new situation, we set about planning an escape from Mountjoy.

Our OC had negotiated with the prison governor to allow us association within our wing, without the presence of jailers, between 4 p.m. and 5 p.m. when jailers had their break and the rest of the prison was on lock down. During this period some of us circulated openly, so the jailers at the end of our wing could see us, while at the other end a few prisoners worked to break through the floor of a treble cell down into the basement. We had a gramophone and some old records. We put on Ravel's 'Bolero' as loud as possible and some of us gathered around the table tennis table, which was outside the treble cell. When a blow was about to be struck to break through into the basement, we'd cheer and shout to add to the noise so the authorities would not hear the hammering. When they eventually got through, scaffolding poles were found stored in the basement from which a ladder could be erected. The next step was to cut some bars to get out of the basement to the outer prison wall. It was decided to try the wall behind the prison bakery as that was close to D Wing. Between the bakery and the outer wall was a blind spot to most of the prison.

On the appointed afternoon, twenty-four of us made our way, in ones and twos, into the treble cell. We went down through the hole into the basement. Carrying lengths of scaffolding, we made our way to the prison wall where the ladder was assembled. Four men at a time were to climb the ladder and slide down the outside of the wall using ropes, made from sheets, tied to the top rung of the ladder. When the first wave started up the makeshift ladder, however, one leg of it broke. The men fell back to the ground and the ladder hit the wall with a very loud clang. This left twenty-four of us stuck between the bakery and the wall. We quickly tried to fix it up again and a few of us managed to clamber up to the top of the wall. What we did not realise, however, was that armed Special Branch detectives were patrolling the outside perimeter. The clang of the ladder against the wall brought a detective running to where we were. When I reached the top he was cocking his sub-machine gun, yelling at us to go back or he would shoot. Being only about 20 feet away, we had little choice. He really looked like he would shoot too.

By now the alarm was blaring. We hurried back into the basement, replaced the scaffolding and made our way back into the prison wing. Almost immediately it was filled with jailers and police. We were bundled into our cells and a big security search was conducted. They did not immediately discover the hole in the treble cell so one of the lads there went down the hole again, out into the compound and proceeded to walk calmly to the main gates. With the prison teeming with detectives, he was let through the first gates. It was only as he was about to go through the last gate to freedom that a jailer recognised him and he was caught. Even though the attempt failed, we had tried. And the buzz of it all was better than simply waiting to be hauled to internment.

We were confined to cells without letters or visits for a few days and then everything returned to the normal prison routine. Those who had been in the treble cell were relocated into single cells. Communication with the outside world resumed and my Mum came to see me regularly. I loved seeing her and enjoyed her wit and her comments on life outside. She brought me news of my sister Pauline nursing in London and of Pat who was still living at home. I tried to keep our chats away from the prison and the IRA because those subjects clearly worried her. She could appear to be carefree but I knew that was only on the surface. Naturally she was fearful that I might be injured, or worse. She was a proud woman with a great spirit. As she used to say sometimes, 'Keep your chin up and walk tall.' My Dad stayed away, still upset with me. A few friends also visited me. Security was tighter and the time dragged, but it was not long until my sentence was up.

3

As each of us was released from Mountjoy and stepped out through the prison gate, we were bundled into army lorries. I was put in a canvas-covered lorry, with long wooden benches along each side. Our belongings were piled in the middle. The rear of the lorry was open. We could see the streets of Dublin as we passed through the city with armed Special Branch following us closely. The journey took about two hours, during which time some of us tried to cut or open the side canvas in another effort to escape, while the volunteers at the back made a show of sightseeing to cover the effort. But the Special Branch car behind kept veering from side to side in order to see along the sides of the lorry. We were unsuccessful but it brightened up the journey.

We were taken to The Curragh, a plain in County Kildare where the British Army previously had a large military complex. The new Free State Army took over the complex for its own military purposes in 1922 when the Free State was established, and prison camps were built there to hold republican prisoners during the Civil War. These camps were built of galvanised iron, like Nissen huts, and referred to as 'Tintown' by republicans. During the Second World War, republicans were interned, that is imprisoned without charge or trial, in some of the camps. British and German military personnel who landed in the state, which was neutral during the war, were also held there in separate camps.

We entered the camp through a complex of barriers, military policemen and gates into a compound comprised of administration, medical, visiting, and military police huts of varying sizes. Going from there into the main prison compound entailed being passed through more barriers, gates and armed military police. The whole camp was surrounded by high barbed-wire fences with watch towers on each corner manned by armed soldiers. All of this enclosed a large area a couple of hundred yards square, where prisoners were held in four accommodation huts. In appearance, the camp resembled POW camps often seen in war films.

We were brought to the administration hut where we were processed in alphabetical order. Consequently, I was one of the last to be dealt with and missed dinner. I was assigned to a temporary hut with about forty other internees. There were no flush toilets, only two cubicles with large buckets at the end of the hut about 30 feet from my bed. After lockup, some prisoners became ill with vomiting and diarrhoea. At first this seemed funny to the unaffected, but soon these too became ill until practically the whole hut was sick. That put a stop to the laughter. All through the night queues of shivering men were frantically waiting to relieve themselves. The stench was appalling. The buckets had to be emptied and replaced several times by the military police that were on guard.

I thought my turn to be ill would surely come, wondering how on earth I could survive years like this. I had heard stories about the internment camps during the war, but nothing had prepared me for this type of existence. I pulled my blanket up over my head to block out some of the stench, curled up and tried to sleep. Whatever the future might hold, I just had to get through this night and hope for the best. Eventually an army doctor came, giving out medicine to the sufferers. Gradually it passed its peak and we got some sleep, of sorts.

Next day I was moved to one of the huts with running water, wash-hand basins and toilets. And I discovered, to my intense relief, that things were much better than that first horrible night. Apparently, with the influx of so many new prisoners, the army cooks had got new pots that morning. Dinner was cooked without boiling out the pots, which meant the storage grease on the metal was cooked into the dinner, resulting in chronic food poisoning and severe diarrhoea. Only four prisoners had escaped that ordeal, those who had arrived after dinner.

I was in Hut 4. Between the door and one end of the hut there were twelve men, including me. As most of us were from Dublin, this area became known as the 'Dublin Republic'. There were four pot-bellied stoves to each hut, the only source of heat. As the camp had not been occupied or maintained since the Germans were there in the mid-1940s, there were cracks in the walls which let in the wind and sometimes the rain.

We had our meals in a dining hut. It was similar to the other huts except it was divided into two sections and furnished with tables and bench seating. The kitchen was manned by army cooks with a serving hatch to the dining area. We provided for ourselves otherwise, serving the meals, washing the dishes and cleaning up, etc. Orderly rotas were established and we looked after ourselves wherever possible.

Each afternoon a mobile shop came into the camp from which we could purchase various essentials using our camp money. The state did not supply us with such basics as soap, toothpaste, polish, washing powder or towels, so we had to purchase them ourselves. Unless we got money from our families, our only source of income was the sale of crafts we made. In the Dublin Republic we pooled our resources; it was funny to hear men discussing which soap powder was the best for washing clothes. There were no washing machines and we did our laundry in the laundry hut, another large galvanised tin structure with occasional hot water.

We had a radio in each section of the hut and could listen to the news and other programmes. This was regulated by consensus;

the volume was controlled likewise. We were allowed books and I read a lot. We also had debates, sing-songs and storytelling. We younger ones engaged in horseplay and pranks, the kind of devilment young men can get up to when confined. We often sat around the stove telling stories, reminiscing about our younger days. Listening to other accounts of school life, I realised that Synge Street Christian Brothers School was not much different to other similar institutions.

The first winter we had no fuel. It was bitterly cold until someone discovered where the turf was stacked when the Germans had been there. That discovery created a flurry of activity as we all pulled back the top sod to reveal the remnants of the original turf stacks. We gathered it all up, got our stoves going and really enjoyed being warm again. After that, the state supplied us with turf and things got better. Our beds comprised of a mattress on three planks resting on two trestles about 9 inches off the floor. We made representations to the International Red Cross, and a few days before the Red Cross delegation was due to inspect the camp, we were supplied with army beds. There was a wash room with toilets and wash-hand basins attached to each hut. The shower hut was a large galvanised tin structure in the compound about 50 yards from the huts. But it was like a lottery trying to get hot water, as each time another person turned on the water it got colder.

These discomforts served to harden us and strengthen us in our resolve to endure and survive. We relieved tension by playing football and basketball, and by jogging around the inside perimeter of the camp. This was defined by a wire about 1 foot high and about 10 feet from the barbed-wire fence, beyond which we stepped at risk of being shot by the sentries in watch towers at each corner. Beyond that high barbed-wire fence was about 6 feet of concertina wire and another high barbed-wire fence. Then there was a wide, deep trench filled with more concertina wire and then another high barbed-wire fence. Beyond that was a footpath where a military policeman patrolled up and down. He was armed with a revolver and hand grenades. Beyond him there were yet more high barbed-wire fences. All the internal camp guards were from the military police. They had red bands on their caps and we referred to them as 'redcaps'. They were like a prison administration. The watch towers were manned by armed soldiers who were not redcaps, with different army units providing sentries for fixed periods. It could happen that one of us might know one of the sentries, who might have been from our home area. Then there would be a surreptitious greeting between sentry and internee so the authorities would not notice.

Walking around the compound one day, there was a shout from a sentry in one of the watch towers. 'Hey Liam! How is it going in there?'

'Mick! When did they bring you down here?' And Liam turned to us, saying, 'That's my brother Mick! Hey Tony, Peter, you know Mick don't you?'

'How're ya, Tony! How're ya, Peter! Good to see yis, how's it in there?'

'Not so bad, Mick. Could be worse. You know how it is.'

'Ah, sure. Ma says hello, Liam. They're all well at home. Take care of yourself.'

There followed a shouted conversation between the two brothers through the barbed wire for about ten minutes. An army squad was spotted marching towards the watch tower, and Liam said, 'We better go now, Mick. Hope you don't get into trouble.'

'Fuck them,' came the reply. 'I'm only talkin' to me brother. See you Liam.'

We moved away as Mick was relieved of his post and escorted away to army quarters. He was transferred to a different unit and did no more sentry duty, which pleased him.

We had our own elected Camp OC, and Camp Council. Each of the four huts had its own OC. We answered only to our own authority and did not speak or communicate directly with the army guards. Our Camp OC was Tomás McCurtain from Cork, a very impressive, big man. His father, also Tomás McCurtain, Lord Mayor of Cork, was murdered by British forces during the War of Independence, or the 'Black and Tan War' as it was sometimes called. Tomás, our OC, had been sentenced to death during the Second World War for the shooting of a detective. He had been held in the 'condemned cell' in Mountjoy, and we learned from him about the conditions he endured when he was sentenced to death. His sentence was commuted to life imprisonment because of pressure on the government from America. He was a wonderful storyteller and very humorous, with a lightness which impressed me, given his background.

Life within the camp was not so bad in some respects. Being with men of like philosophy was educational. Classes were organised by the Camp Council. These were held during the day, leaving us to our own pursuits in the evenings after lockup. We could study Irish as well as History, Politics, Sociology and Economics. These classes were held openly. The ones on Guerrilla Warfare and Engineering were held surreptitiously. All of this training brought closer the possibility that I might, at some time, go on active service. The theory of guerrilla warfare was fine, but how would I be on active service? That question troubled me and also some of my young friends. I felt that I could fight, if needs be, but could I actually kill someone? This serious question was discussed among us. For myself, I knew I could not kill someone in cold blood, so to speak. But if I were on an action, facing an enemy trying to kill me, I felt that would be different. I could handle that. Even as we discussed the question and I pondered it, within myself I hoped that I would never be faced with it.

After a few months we were allowed make crafts in our huts. Leatherwork and matchstick models were the usual pastimes. I made up a small loom and made criosanna with the assistance of Monty, the only Belfast man in the Dublin Republic. Criosanna are woven woollen belts in the Gaelic tradition. We had to purchase the raw materials ourselves, but the sale of our crafts made us some pocket money. We were not allowed actual money but the army issued camp money, being metal discs denoting different values and with 'Curragh' stamped on them. Money left in for us or sent to us was held 'on account' by the authorities. Provided we had money in our account we could draw camp money. Criosanna were popular at the time and those we made in the camp sold well. I even got orders by the dozen from a shop in Connemara.

My Mum came to visit regularly. She was naturally worried about me. There was always a military policeman supervising and the quality of the visits often depended on how easy going he was. As a result, sometimes it was painful being with her on visits. But our visits could be cheerful, filled with news from home.

After about six months' internment my Dad came to visit me. It was the first time I'd seen him since the Bridewell. I was glad he had come. Our visit went well, until he asked me the name of the army officer who was in charge of the camp. I told him I didn't know because we had nothing to do with the military manning the camp. I explained how we had our own leadership, our OC and Camp Council, and went on to tell him that our OC was Tomás McCurtain. At that my Dad, who was normally a calm man, exploded. 'That murderer! That fella tried to kill me one time.' He then proceeded to tell me that during the Second World War there was a riot in Mountjoy Prison. He was called up there on duty, as part of the reinforcements. During the fracas, Tomás had thrown a big jam jar, narrowly missing him and injuring a Garda inspector. He was convinced Tomás aimed at him, and there was nothing I could say to placate him, at least not on this visit. My attitude did not help pacify him, as I insisted that I trusted my OC and would not hear anything bad against him. My Dad left in disgust. The whole episode upset me also. My every action seemed to hurt him – first my arrest and now this. I loved him and respected him and did not want to cause him upset, yet at the same time I was firm in following my own road, which was not his.

A day or two later I told Tomás about what my father had said. He recalled the incident in Mountjoy but said that it was not my Dad he aimed at but an inspector. Apparently this inspector was urging his squad on from behind to attack the barricade. My Dad reached back and grabbed him by the collar, pulling him forward and telling him to lead the way and they would follow. As he pulled the inspector forward, McCurtain let fly the jam jar, hitting him on the head and knocking him out. And that was the end of that sortie. Tomás told me that he had always admired the Garda who pulled the inspector to the front, as the inspector was hiding behind his own men while urging them to attack. I was amazed about that connection between my Dad and McCurtain, but I did not get to talk about it with my Dad until after my release, as he did not visit me again.

Apart from my immediate family, no other relations visited me or wrote to me while I was interned. No one else in the family was republican, as far as I knew. Perhaps they disapproved of me, or perhaps they were afraid of being supportive or of being seen to be supportive. There was also the fact that writing to an internee would bring the writer to the attention of Special Branch. Not all of the men interned were in the IRA, and the possibility of also being interned was a powerful incentive not to associate with an internee by writing or visiting. Grandad passed away while I was interned. I was not told at the time, as my family did not want to give me the bad news when I was locked up. I would not have been able to attend his funeral. But still, I think I would have preferred to have been told when it happened, instead of much later when I was released.

Exercise was very important, and I made a point of walking for a few hours every day, regardless of the weather. There was a well-worn path around the camp perimeter, and there were always men walking in pairs or threes or alone. It was an unspoken rule that if a man wished to walk alone, nobody would intrude on his solitude. Sometimes as I walked I would look across the plain in the direction of Rathangan where my grandparents lived on their small farm. I would remember the wonderful times I had there with them, and such memories and my daydreams around them broke the monotony of walking alongside barbed wire in never-ending circumferences of the prison camp.

One evening I got severe pains in my side. The hut OC called for medical assistance and the camp doctor on duty came and examined me. He diagnosed constipation and gave me laxatives. But I knew I was not constipated and so did not take the laxatives. I spent the night curled up in my bed in severe pain. The next morning Dr Cahill came to the hut to see me. He was a captain. The doctor who examined me the evening before held higher rank but that did not stop Cahill giving out hell about his incompetence. I was taken by army ambulance to The Curragh Military Hospital with acute appendicitis. I was kept under observation that day and had my appendix removed the following morning.

The night before my operation, a nurse came to me and told me that the surgeon was very good and that 'his hands have been blessed by the Pope'. Then she asked if I wished to see the priest, but I declined.

'But you are going under the knife in the morning. It could be dangerous.'

'But you told me the surgeon's hands were blessed by the Pope,' I replied. 'So how could it be dangerous?'

With that she flounced off. I didn't mean to upset her, but I was no longer a Catholic and had no time for priests or the church, which had excommunicated us all anyway when we were in Mountjoy. The operation was successful, though the size of the scar caused me to think the surgeon could be a butcher as well as a surgeon. The best part of being in the hospital was being attended to by women after being isolated from them since my arrest. After being locked up for over a year, the nurses and ward attendants all seemed beautiful, and it was a treat having them around and talking with them.

Internees were held in the detention ward in the hospital. All the windows were barred and there was a steel cage inside the door. Two armed military police were stationed in the cage, one with a Gustav sub-machine gun and the second with a revolver. Anybody entering or leaving the ward was checked in and out by them. There was a locked gate from the cage into the ward. There were six beds, while the toilets and bathroom area was through a door across the ward from the cage. The guards could only see the passageway and not into any of the cubicles. We were given a grey night shirt and slippers to wear in the ward. Our clothes were in a closet. Being tall, my night shirt only reached to my knees, much to the amusement of the two wards maids who came to clean and polish in the mornings. They were local girls – civilians, not military. Sometimes the guards were a bit lax, more interested in the sports page of the newspaper than in us. I would go into the bathroom area to chat to the girls and have a bit of fun with them. It was a pleasant interlude away from the tensions of camp life.

About ten days after being returned to the camp I was walking about when a football was kicked towards me. I instinctively reached out for it and my wound opened. I reported to the doctor. Captain Cahill was on duty that day and he ordered that I be taken back to hospital. As he wrote the Order, he said, 'I know what happened. You did this just to get back to the young ones cleaning the ward. You better not get any of them pregnant.' And he laughed, seeing my embarrassment.

When I was brought back to the hospital there was only one other patient in the detention ward, Pádraig MacLogan, who had been president of Sinn Féin when he was interned. He was a veteran of long years in the struggle as far back as the War of Independence. He was quite old and frail, but one could still feel the steel in him. We were in beds each side of the fireplace. As it was cold, they kept a nice fire burning which made the ward quite snug, even with the armed military watching us. I was able to spend a little time with the wards maids again. We had some fun and no one became pregnant.

One evening, Colonel McInerney, the army surgeon in charge of the hospital, came in with another elderly man, not in uniform. To my surprise, when this man approached MacLogan's bed he came to attention and saluted him. The colonel left, and Pádraig invited this man to sit between the two beds in front of the fire. He introduced him to me, but for the life of me I cannot remember his name. They chatted and reminisced about old times, in particular the War of Independence and the Civil War. They had been comrades during the 'Tan' war but had taken opposite sides in the Civil War. This visitor was a retired senior Free State officer, apparently a brigadier, I think.

They spoke of how the occupation of the Four Courts in Dublin by the IRA brought the division between Treaty and Anti-Treaty forces to a serious crisis. Britain was pressurising the Free State government to attack the republicans and sort out the matter. Michael Collins, who was in command of the Free State Army, secretly arranged a meeting in The Curragh between senior Free State and senior IRA officers to try to reach a solution. Pádraig MacLogan and his visitor had been delegates on either side. From listening to their discussion it became clear that Collins had offered to surreptitiously provide weapons, explosives and funds for the IRA to carry on the struggle against the British in the North, on condition that they would leave the Four Courts and only carry on the fight on British-occupied territory.

Collins' offer was conveyed to the IRA leadership occupying the Four Courts. They were sceptical and asked that Collins himself come to the Four Courts to convince them that it was not a ploy to get them to give up the struggle. Collins was very much in the public domain at that time and could not enter the Four Courts secretly or be seen to do so. The negotiations continued in secret between both sides, but unfortunately they failed. The Free State bombarded the Four Courts and the Civil War resulted. These negotiations were not officially sanctioned by the Free State government. The Free State officers were negotiating for Michael Collins in a genuine attempt to avert civil war.

It was quite an experience for me, listening to these two old comrades speak about that time and to observe their grief and sadness, having failed in that effort. It must have been about 11 p.m. when the colonel collected the ex-Free State officer. He and Pádraig parted as friends. When Pádraig lay back in his hospital bed he seemed to be in meditation and did not speak to me again that night. I was profoundly touched by these two old veterans and their conversation.

It was a strict rule in the IRA that no matter what rank a member held on the outside, once he was arrested he reverted to being a simple volunteer. IRA rank did not carry into prison. This meant that the OC was always the senior officer within the place of imprisonment, and so it was in the camp. In 1958 a number of senior officers were arrested and interned in The Curragh, the chief of staff among them. Up until then escape was discouraged by the leadership outside, the same people who were themselves now interned. When they found themselves on the inside, some of them began to agitate and criticise the Camp OC for not organising an escape, contrary to their own position when they were on the outside. This created tensions within the camp and almost a complete split. At our weekly camp meetings, men whom I had grown to respect engaged in verbal attacks on each other and on our OC.

Eventually, at one meeting I spoke up and let them know how I felt about their behaviour. I told them that they were letting themselves down, as well as the movement and the rest of us in the camp. I asked if this was their idea of showing leadership, or were they just unable to do their time. Were we prepared to split the camp to satisfy their inflated egos? I reminded them of the army rule: no matter what their rank was outside, when they came into the camp they reverted to being volunteers, the same as the rest of us. I spoke from my heart and pulled no punches. When I had finished, there was silence and considerable unease among the whingers. It shook them that a young volunteer would stand up to them. And while it did not altogether stop them, they toned down a bit. A lot of people thanked me for speaking up, and I was glad that I had.

The whole episode was a good lesson for me. I had respected those people, and had held expectations of them that were too high. I had not understood that the defects of character which the rest of us held were also held by them. I learned to observe more closely how people behaved, and to be aware when ego played a big part in their actions. It showed me clearly the risk of the 'follow the leader' attitude that has pervaded our history. It is better to follow the principle than to follow the leader.

Rory Brady and Dave O'Connell were in our hut, and a plan was made by the Camp Council for their escape. I think they were chosen to go because of their experience. Football was played in the sports compound, adjacent to the main camp. There was a gate and bridge to this compound, and the usual watch towers, etc. A football match was arranged between two huts, and all the prisoners went to the sports compound one afternoon. I was assigned to be one of a group covering Rory and Dave as they were to slip under the wire. The game started, and we stood at the chosen place about midway between the two sentry posts. The redcap on the footpath between the barbed-wire fences moved further along so that he could see the game, which was being played fast and furious and to much cheering and shouting from all sides. A pre-arranged fracas broke out on the playing pitch, drawing the attention of the sentries even more. We pretended to be part of the shouting, cheering crowd, but at the same time two of us lifted the bottom of the wire. Rory and Dave slid under, squirming through the long grass and into the concertina wire, covering themselves with a camouflaged blanket.

When the game was over we had to cross back into the main compound and satisfy the head count on the way in. We all piled through in a big bunch and in the middle two dummy heads were held up. We got through no bother. The dummy heads were made from papier-mâché. They had painted faces and real hair and were very realistic. A number of men had their hair cut the previous day and the leavings provided the hair for the dummies, which were modelled on Rory and Dave. There were some audible sighs of relief as we headed back to the huts. Rory and Dave lay still until dark. There were no sentries in that area once all the prisoners had returned to the main compound, so once the coast was clear Rory and Dave cut their way out and made their way to the road, where they were picked up by a car.

Back in the hut the two dummies were placed in their beds. A couple of other men were in bed as well, so it did not seem unusual. When the count was called, we stood at our beds. 'Sputnik' was doing the count. Sputnik was our nickname for a redcap sergeant who was short and rotund and not a bad sort. As he was doing the count we were all talking about the football game, laughing and heckling him as we usually did at this time. Sputnik noticed nothing wrong, and the count passed without incident. It was a great evening, although a little anxious as we waited to see if the outside alarm would go off. But the night remained quiet, and the following morning the dummies were burned in the stoves.

It was not until the second night that Rory and Dave were missed. The state did not know when or how they had escaped – and they were not re-captured. Afterwards, security became stricter. Guards came into each hut during the night and made a count. If a prisoner had his head under the covers, they would pull the covers back to see the man in the bed. This caused considerable aggravation and disturbance during the night.

Some time later there was another mad attempt to break out in daylight. A group rushed the wire in the mistaken belief that the sentries would not open fire. They were wrong. It was fortunate that no one was killed. Five internees were injured by stun grenades, thrown by the redcap on guard between the sentry boxes.

There was one other successful escape. Big Vincent and his pal Larry decided to go out from the detention ward in the military hospital. They managed to pull a radiator back from the wall and make a hole. Jimmy Kelly from Dublin was also in the hospital at the time. They decided that he should stay behind in the ward to allay suspicion while they got away. One evening they went in to the bathroom area, pulled back the radiator, opened the way out and slipped through. Jimmy waited for some time to be sure they were away, before following them out. The irony of this was that Jimmy was the only one to make good the escape and was not re-captured. Vincent and Larry never made it away from the Curragh area and were captured the following day. Jimmy had hitched a ride in a lorry and told the driver that he was an escaped internee. The driver, also a Dub, hid him and got him safely to Dublin, where he was given refuge.

Any internee could be released if he signed an undertaking to support the state and not engage in any subversive activities in future. As a matter of principle we rejected that possibility. Some men, unable to do their time or due to family pressures, signed out and were quietly spirited from the camp. A man might go on a visit and not return, and later the redcaps would collect his belongings. A man might sign the form and then the authorities might not release him for some days, which must have been horrendous for the poor man. Signing out meant that he had turned away from his comrades, and the movement. Having to stay in the camp, not knowing when or if he would be released, and not knowing if we would learn of his action before his release, must have been nerve-wracking for him. Sometimes a man would be released without having signed out, and a rumour would circulate that he had done so. These events were very demoralising for the remainder of the prisoners. But we did learn more about the deviousness of our captors.

Very gradually the state released internees, often in ones and twos. Sometimes days or even weeks would pass without any releases, which increased the tension among us. Everyone wanted out. And whenever an officer entered the camp to speak with McCurtain, we all waited with bated breath to see if anyone was going out.

I was released in March 1959, by which time I believe only twenty-four men were held in the camp after I left. I was driven out to the main road and given a ticket for the bus to Dublin. I was not yet 21 years old.

4

Upon arrival in Dublin I went to my parents' house. They were very glad to see me and made me very welcome. It was really nice being with my family again. Pauline was still nursing in London and Pat was living at home. My Dad was open and friendly with me, and my Mum seemed to think I had been starved in The Curragh as she cooked and baked and delighted in seeing my appetite. It was a treat being home and eating her home cooking and her wonderful scones and tarts.

Being free was terrific. Simply walking through the streets of Dublin with the hustle and bustle of people going about their business and listening to their voices was very exciting. I loved every minute of it. My release was reported in the newspapers and my former employer contacted me and offered me my job back. I started work the following Monday, which made me feel good. Work was scarce that time and it was a real bonus having my old job back.

After release from prison, if a volunteer wanted to resume activity in the IRA it was up to him to make contact with the local unit. The problem was that I could not find the Dublin unit. I spoke to other ex-prisoners. Some did not want to know and others, like me, could not locate the unit. I went to Gerry McCarthy, an old-timer who had been interned with us. A tough old man who had devoted his life to the struggle, Gerry told me that there was no Dublin unit any more. I was surprised, and asked him what I should do. He suggested that if I wanted to do something useful I could re-establish the unit; gather together those who wanted to be active and then contact him and he would connect with someone in HQ.

Over the next few weeks I went around Dublin after work and at weekends contacting comrades whom I knew from the camp and before the camp. Some were no longer interested. Others were not prepared to commit themselves to the struggle and the possibility of going to prison again, or worse. For them the prison experience was enough. That was understandable, although some tried to avoid me as if ashamed they could not continue in the struggle. Even some of the senior people, who had almost split the camp advocating more action, now did not want to know. Nevertheless, there was still a hard core of people willing to continue. And when I had them drawn together I notified Gerry, who duly organised a meeting with someone from HQ. The Dublin unit was re-established, and I was given the job as OC. This surprised me, as I had no experience other than as a volunteer. I was advised on what the job entailed and decided to do my best. Being so immersed in IRA work, however, I had no time or inclination to attend Sinn Féin meetings. My focus had changed.

Between working during the day and organising in the evenings I was extremely busy, with hardly a moment to myself. Occasionally I would have a few pints with pals and maybe go to a dance. The campaign limped along with great difficulty. My job as OC was to continue organising the Dublin unit, so I appointed an intelligence officer, training officer, recruiting officer, finance officer and a quartermaster to be members of the unit staff, and they in turn set about organising their various departments with my help. We had few weapons so we set about trying to locate equipment which seemed to have disappeared while we were imprisoned. It all came together slowly, and it took a lot of my energy. I had to contact sympathisers to set up safe houses for holding parades (meetings), and we established ground rules to guard against being followed to such houses. Special Branch kept a close eye on a lot of us, especially those among us who had been imprisoned. Instructions were issued to all volunteers that if they thought they were being followed, not to think they could lose their tail but to abort their effort to get to a parade and go elsewhere.

All this activity, immediately after my release, began to have a negative effect on me. I became very restless in myself as I seemed to have no life of my own. After four months of this I spoke to my employer, who graciously gave me two weeks' holidays. I packed a rucksack and hitch-hiked to the west.

I spent days on the hills on my own, walking the Twelve Bens and then the Maamturks. It felt good being out alone on the hills. I had no tent but I had two groundsheets and a good sleeping bag. I was happy sleeping out, especially as the weather was fine. I rigged one of the groundsheets as a sort of canopy in case of rain, and slept comfortably on the heather beside a stream.

It was wonderful waking up in the early morning to the sun rising above the hills, listening to the stream gurgling and the birds singing. Hearing the lark and seeing him high in the air was a particular joy. Then I would get out of my sleeping bag, naked, fill my billycan, light my Primus and wash in the stream. The cold water was invigorating, and after I got dressed my whole body would be tingling. Then I would make breakfast with whatever provisions I had, after which I'd pack my rucksack and set off again.

One day I went down to the road near Maam Bridge and came upon two Dublin girls hitch-hiking to the hostel on the shores of Killary Harbour, the only deep-water fjord in Ireland. As we were chatting they hitched a lift from a big black Dodge. I knew it was an official state car and would have a Special Branch detective as its driver. It stopped and they ran to it. The front-seat passenger got out and beckoned me to come on. I recognised him as Niall Blaney, parliamentary secretary to Seán Lemass, then Minister for Commerce. 'Come on young man, there's plenty of room,' he said as he put our rucksacks into the boot. I was nervous being in that car, with Special Branch driving and a senior politician beside him. It was a very warm, sunny day. The driver had his jacket folded on the bench seat next to him and I could just see the butt of his handgun when I leaned forward. Blaney and the girls chatted away. He was very knowledgeable and informative about the locality we were driving through.

On the way into Leenane the car stopped at a large house which I realised was the Garda station. Blaney went into the building and came back out with a Garda sergeant. I felt myself tighten up, not knowing what was about to unfold. But Blaney simply gave the sergeant a bundle of election posters from the boot of the car. The girls were very impressed with Blaney, who was very personable. While he was out of the car they quizzed the detective as to who he was. He pretended that Blaney was a lord, and he was his chauffeur. When he got back into the car the detective told him the story, in Irish. We drove on, and they continued the pretence. They dropped us off at the road to the hostel, and as we parted I could not resist saying, 'Thanks Mr Blaney', and enjoyed seeing their faces drop.

I spent some days at the hostel at Killary, mixing with people. One day I walked to Tully Cross to buy groceries and had a couple of pints and a chat with some locals. When I got back to the hostel about 9 p.m. it was in darkness. As I entered I was greeted by voices in the half-light. I lit the oil lamp and saw that someone had tried, unsuccessfully, to light the fire. I quickly got it going, muttering to myself about people who could not even light an oil lamp or a fire. There were people from America, England, Germany, France and New Zealand there that night. All from advanced societies, but none of them could light an oil lamp or get a turf fire going! I began to see the funny side of it and went to the kitchen to cook some food. I had bought a big steak, mushrooms and onions. As I prepared to cook my dinner, two of the women from New Zealand came in and offered to cook for me in return for my lighting the fire. We chatted while they cooked, and we ate the food together. It turned out to be a very pleasant evening.

The next morning, Festy, the warden of the hostel, loaned me a currach, which is a lightly framed canvas-covered open boat, tar-coated to keep it watertight. With the two New Zealanders and an American couple on board I rowed out from the little harbour. A currach can be very skittish on the water, and although very seaworthy it requires delicate handling. Skilfully rowing a currach takes practice. I had observed local boatmen handling their currachs and found that I could manage one fairly well. We had fun when the others took turns trying to row it in a straight line. We crossed Killary and ran the boat on to the sand at a lovely beach on the Mayo side and we had a picnic on the beach. I walked to a house in the distance where I knew 'poteen', the local home brew, was made and bought two bottles. When I returned to the others I stored the poteen safely in the boat. Then we pushed off, rowing for the hostel. There were hand lines in the currach and we trolled for mackerel as we rowed. We caught over a dozen, much to the excitement of the women, especially when the fish were jumping and wriggling in the bottom of the boat.

We got back safely and pulled the currach out of the water. When we had it unloaded we turned it upside down, as was the custom. While the others went in to the hostel to cook the mackerel, I brought some of the fresh fish and a bottle of poteen as gifts to Festy for lending me the boat. Back in the hostel we had a good feed of mackerel and potatoes. And we partied afterwards on the poteen, sitting around the fire, telling stories and sharing experiences. A good time was had by all. By the end of the evening I was the only one standing. I finished what was left of the poteen and went to my bunk in the annex.

The following day the other people in the hostel moved on, except for Sally from New Zealand, who decided to stay a few more days before going to rejoin her friends in Dublin. We spent that first day walking along the shore. We were the only people in the hostel. That night she moved in to the small annex where I was sleeping. The hostel only had bunk beds, so we put two mattresses on the floor and slept together. We had three days together before she had to head off to Dublin to reconnect with her friends. I was due back in Dublin the following week and we arranged to meet there.

Those days I did not have any particular girlfriend. I dated occasionally, but between working during the day and organising during the evenings the occasional date suited me best. Dating someone on a regular basis would have posed the problem of how to explain my other activities, which were, out of necessity, secret. Sally spent a couple of evenings with me in Dublin before leaving Ireland to continue her tour of Europe. I returned to work and to my activities as OC of the Dublin unit. I spent my weekends walking the hills, usually alone, or else in training sessions in the same hills.

After work on paydays some of the staff went to the pub across the road for a few pints. I was invited along. At first I would just have an orange, but then one evening decided to have a pint of stout like my workmates. I liked it, and had a second before leaving for home. Cycling uphill to Inchicore seemed easier than before, and I was happy as I went. When I got home I made no mention of drinking, which did not seem significant to me at the time. After that I would have the occasional pint or two and that was that, although I very much enjoyed the pub atmosphere of banter and chats and sometime serious conversations.

The intelligence section discovered that some of our missing weapons were in a particular house in Dublin. This house was occupied by a young man and his widowed mother. He had been on the fringes of the movement and was now part of a dissident group which was trying to organise itself. We figured he would not hand over the weapons and we devised a plan for their recovery.

We arranged a 'Special Branch' raid on the house early one morning. That is to say, two cars similar to what the Special Branch used drew up to the house, with four tall volunteers in each car dressed in suits and shirts and ties. When the woman of the house answered the door, we entered, producing a warrant to search the house. The young man was taken from his bed and brought downstairs. At first he was defiant and cocky, but we knew the good cop, bad cop routine, having experienced it ourselves. And soon he crumbled. While the other 'detectives' searched the house, I was in the kitchen with the young man and his mother. I put the kettle on and made tea and spoke to the young man, advising him to get sense; not to risk going to prison, losing his job and causing his dear mother huge distress. Of course she, poor woman, also pleaded with him. We told him we would give him a chance and not take him away if he would undertake to leave his group. He finally agreed.

The weapons, discovered in the attic, were loaded into the two cars. We left the young man and his mother greatly relieved with their good fortune. Intelligence kept an eye on him for a while just to see if he kept to his word, which he did. As far as his group was concerned, the house had been raided by Special Branch and their weapons confiscated. Our quartermaster took charge of the weapons, which were used for training purposes.

Week-long training camps were regularly organised in the Wicklow Mountains. Most of these went off without incident, but one had to be aborted. We had the use of a Volkswagen pickup, and under a tarpaulin in the back were all the food supplies for the camp. Myself and the camp cook were also in the back under the tarpaulin. The training officer for the camp, a man who was on the run, was in front with the volunteer driver. Driving through a village on the way to the mountains, the pickup was flagged down by a Garda. He was not satisfied with our driver's explanation of his journey towards the mountains at 6.30 p.m. on a Friday and decided to check the back. He tried to lift the tarpaulin but it was tied down. Just as he was about to climb up on to the back of the pickup, our driver drove off and he fell back on to the road.

We knew we had no more than twenty minutes to get off the road before the alarm kicked in. We turned back to the Dublin suburbs by another route and put a contingency plan into action. Driving to a safe house in Drimnagh, we quickly unloaded the pickup. Someone went to phone it in as having been stolen, and then the pickup was to be driven out to the main road, where the driver was to leave it and go home immediately. He would only have about five minutes to spare. But, deciding to go further than instructed, he took too long about it and was arrested, and spent three months in Mountjoy as a result. The groceries we unloaded were distributed among the needy families in the area and they were well pleased with the bonanza.

Although I didn't spend much time there, it was nice living at home. I got on well with my family and it was a happy house. Pat seemed content in his job as a barman, and my Mum ran the household in her competent, happy way, as always. My Dad had retired from the Gardaí and my parents were living on his pension. Dad sometimes went to the local pub to meet an old friend and have a couple of pints. One evening I walked down the road with him as I was heading into town. We came to the pub and I offered to buy him a pint. He was a bit surprised that I had started drinking, but made little of it. We went in, and it was really nice being with him chatting companionably. After sharing two pints together he suggested it was enough and I headed into town. He enjoyed his pint but knew when he had enough.

Two of Dad's brothers, Mick and Peter, called to the house one night about midnight with news that their mother had passed away. After a brief discussion my Dad decided to wait until morning before heading to my grandparents' place in County Kildare. Mick and Peter went that night and Dad followed on the first bus in the morning. Mick and Peter were up all night at the wake, and when Dad arrived he was fresh and ready to do what was needed, which was typical of him. Later that day I borrowed a car and drove Mum and Pat down.

There was a large gathering at my grandmother's house where she was waked. I met aunts, uncles and cousins I had not seen for years. My grandmother was the local historian, and was almost ninety when she passed on. Uncle Francis, a Franciscan monk, accompanied by two Franciscan priests who had attended my grandmother, told me of her final days. For over a week before she died she had been continuously asking to speak to me. She had wanted to tell me about two of her granduncles, silversmiths by trade. They had been United Irishmen who fought in the rebellion of 1798. After their capture by English forces they were publicly hanged in Naas. Since that time I was the only republican in our family and she wanted to pass their story on to me. I became very angry that I had not been sent for, to hear what my grandmother wanted to tell me from her death bed. I had to leave for a few hours to contain myself and not cause a scene.

It was also my grandmother's wish that I lead the cortege behind the hearse. My borrowed car could be hard to start sometimes, but fortunately the church was on a hill and I was able to park in a strategic position in case I had to freewheel down to start it. Thankfully the car gave no trouble and everything went smoothly. My grandmother was laid to rest alongside Grandad. And that was consoling for us all, I think. At the cemetery I could see how sad my Dad was, and I felt for him. I was sad too, but also grateful to my grandmother for wanting to talk to me in her final days. On the drive back to Dublin with my parents I thought a lot about what my grandmother might have told me. At least I knew that she would have approved of my path.

5

From time to time, volunteers would be chosen to join an active service unit in the North. I realised that my role was to help to organise the training of volunteers, but I became unhappy with that. I was uneasy about others going while I had to stay behind. Those circumstances changed, however, when Special Branch detectives spotted me in the company of a comrade who was 'on the run'. They gave chase. We managed to elude them, but this meant that I was then also on the run.

After a few weeks we were spotted again and this time we were arrested. We were charged, once again, with failing to account for our movements and as a result I spent another three months in Mountjoy. On the evening of my release I went to a dance with a few pals, and afterwards I brought a young woman home to a block of flats near Sandymount on the south-east of the city. Having checked that her family were all in bed, she brought me in to the sitting room. Warning me to be very quiet, we made out on the carpet. After a while I needed to go to the toilet and she told me where it was. On my way back I opened a door thinking it was to the sitting room, only to find it was a closet. The light came on when I opened the door and, to my shock, I saw what looked like a dark blue police coat hanging there. I quietly shut the door and found my way back to the sitting room. I casually mentioned that I had opened the wrong door and wondered about the blue overcoat. She said it belonged to her brother, who was a warder in Mountjoy Prison. She told me his name, and I knew which one he was. Not a bad jailer, but a jailer nevertheless. After getting out of Mountjoy that day I did not want such a close connection to the place, even though she was an attractive young woman.

I got out of there as quickly as I could, agreeing to meet her later in the week. But I had no intention of making that date. It was after three o'clock in the morning and I had a long walk ahead of me to Kilmainham on the west of the city. When I came out of the complex to the street I noticed a car with two men parked nearby. I walked towards the city, and it followed me at my walking pace. 'Special Branch,' I thought. After failing in my efforts to hail a taxi, I turned around and approached the car. The detective in the passenger seat rolled down his window.

'Looks like you are going to follow me all the way home?'

'Yes, that's right,' he replied.

'In that case, you may as well give me a lift, saving my tired legs. And you'll be able to go home yourselves earlier than if you have to trail after me.'

They looked at each other, and with a big grin the detective reached behind him and opened the rear door. 'Hop in. If you don't mind, we don't either.'

They dropped me off beside my parents' house and we parted amicably. I was glad to get to bed and sleep. I was sure they were also glad to get home earlier than they had expected.

A few days later I received instructions not to get a job but to be ready to go on active service at short notice. I was supposed to get an allowance to live on in the meantime, but this was very little and sporadic. Nevertheless, there were some light interludes. One evening I went out with a few friends from the movement to a party. The women, Clarrie and Muriel, suggested we hail a horse-drawn cab. As we went across town, there was a loud 'bang, bang' and a dishevelled man ran out on the street after our cab. He held a large key like a gun, pointing it at us and yelling, 'bang, bang'. And we laughingly leaned out the windows, pointed our fingers and banged back to him. Everybody on the street was laughing at the spectacle, some joining in the banging. Then he hopped onto the platform of a bus going the other way and his 'bang, bang' faded into the distance. His running through the streets shooting at vehicles and people with his key was seen as harmless fun by Dublin's society. Everyone loved 'Bang Bang', but very few knew him. The poor man lived in squalor in a tenement basement room. When I later heard about his death I wondered if perhaps he was attempting to express himself, beyond anything we may have considered.

On Christmas Eve morning 1960 I had only seven pence to my name and no prospect of any relief. Rather than sit in the house, I walked into town. The city centre was bustling with shoppers and aglow with lights and decorations, which was all a matter to me, being destitute. I wouldn't be able to buy any presents for my parents or my brother Pat. I was supposed to meet friends that afternoon in Madigan's of North Earl Street for a few pints but I knew that was not on for me. Since having my first drink I had learned the protocol of the pubs; each person bought their round in turn. Without having at least the price of a pint, the 'latch-opener' as it was called, I could not face into the pub. My friends would make me welcome, and carry me if I had no money. But my pride would not let me go that way.

As I was walking along Westmorland Street I heard my name being called and turned to find Tom Doyle greeting me. Tom was an old-timer who had been interned in The Curragh in the 1940s, as well as when I was there. He was a very solid, likable man who was then general secretary of the Workers' Union of Ireland. He invited me to Bewley's for coffee and a chat and I accepted, conscious that I had no way to even offer to pay. When we left Bewley's he suggested I walk with him to his office on Parnell Square. We chatted along the way, and when we arrived he invited me into his office where he wrote a cheque for £10. He asked his secretary to cash it, and handed me two crisp £5 notes. 'Go on, take it. You deserve it, and I can afford it. Enjoy yourself. And Happy Christmas to you! See you later; I still have a bit of work to do here.'

I thanked him, shook his hand and left his building, delighted with my change of fortune. I was able to buy little presents for my parents and my brother Pat, and even meet my friends in the afternoon. I had a good Christmas, thanks to the generosity of Tom Doyle.

After Christmas I was sent to the border area and joined a unit operating in Fermanagh and Armagh. It was a very difficult time for us. We could not use the roads, so when we moved we walked cross-country. We could only travel in darkness, and even then we had to move carefully, as sometimes the B Specials – the RUC Reserve, who were loyalist and sectarian – would lie out at night hoping to ambush us. In daylight hours we stayed in safe houses, if we were lucky. When we could not reach such a house we stayed in dugouts or even in derelict ruins, as needs might be. There were a few close calls, where RUC and British troops passed so close to where I was hiding that I could see them and hear what they were saying. But they passed on and I was very relieved that I was not discovered.

I had been issued with good boots but these deteriorated rapidly in the harsh, wet winter conditions. One time, going through a gap between fields coming on daylight, I saw how distinctive my boot tracks were – the sort of thing that could alert a B Man or loyalist to our presence in an area – so I got rid of them and instead got a pair of Wellingtons from a local man. Better not to leave any tracks that might be different to what was usual. If there was snow we could not move about at all, as our tracks in the snow would be too obvious and a giveaway. I remember having to spend a week in an unused room of a safe house with another volunteer to avoid anyone seeing us. When someone called to the house we had to be very quiet. We could not light a fire, as the smoke from a previously unused chimney might draw comment. We were very cold the whole week we were there, so were glad when the thaw came and we could get out again.

We were visited by a representative from GHQ, who apparently noticed I was wearing Wellingtons. Later, when I was in a safe house with three comrades, our OC arrived with money to purchase boots for me. The four of us were smokers and we had no cigarettes. The OC did not smoke. He handed me £2.10 to get the boots. As we sat around a table looking at the money it was commented that it would buy a lot of cigs if only I did not need boots. The idea was bandied about for a few minutes and I agreed that I would manage in my wellies and we would get cigs with the money. The OC objected that the money was for boots not cigs but by this time we smokers were determined and we got our host to get cigs for us. The following week I was given boots by a farmer – the sort local men wore – and everyone was happy; we got the boots as well as the cigarettes.

A lot of our time was spent gathering information about RUC and British Army movements in our area of operations. Sometimes we would set up an ambush, only to find that the patrol would not arrive that night or had switched its route and gone another way. Lying out watching a crossroads or bridge during a cold, wet winter night was no fun – and it was morale sapping if no useful information was gathered. On one occasion five of us were in a shed about 100 yards from the road where we hoped to set up an ambush when a tramp came upon us. He had intended to sleep in the shed. One of our volunteers was left watching the tramp while the rest of us made our way to our positions by the road. The patrol did not come our way. And after lying in wait most of the night we had to pull back as dawn was approaching.

Back at the shed, the tramp, lying on straw in one corner, agreed not to tell anyone about seeing us. Then he asked, 'Who are you lads?'

'The IRA.'

'Do you get paid for doing this?'

'No, we are volunteers.'

There was a pause, before the tramp replied, 'Ah, well, sure I suppose it helps you pass the time.'

We laughed, and went on our way. He was in his own world and far distant from ours. As we went cross-country to a safe base I got to thinking that there are probably as many little worlds as there are people in the big one.

One evening, myself and another volunteer were nearly caught by the Gardaí just south of the border. We got away, however, but knowing there would be a big search for us we split up and went to warn other comrades so we could all move out of the immediate area and the inevitable cordon of military and police. By the time I reached the Monaghan–Armagh road the area was saturated with security forces. But I was able to slip across and warn my comrades, and the search proved unsuccessful. All my previous walking across hills and country stood to me then, beyond what I would have imagined when I first took it up. The odds were against us. We had very little resources, apart from our stubborn resolve to continue. For myself, I did not even consider packing it all in, even though I was well aware that I could be caught anytime. And that's what inevitably happened.

Travelling cross-country another night we were jumped on by a patrol of armed men. Lights were shone on us and there was shouting. I think they were as surprised as we were, and in the confusion we ran away, with the men giving furious chase. We ran down a lane between fields. It was a dark night, and being long-legged I passed my two comrades and ran into a metal gate across the lane. I hit it with my right thigh with such force that the gate and its posts fell down, with me tangled in it. I scrambled to my feet and took off again, some of my pursuers having gained ground on me. I leapt over a hedge but the field was lower than the lane and I landed heavily. Again I made it to my feet, but about 50 yards further on my leg collapsed under me and I was pounced on by three of my pursuers.

That's when I learned that they were Garda detectives. I was taken to the road and sat with my captors on a high grassy bank at the side. Some time later more detectives arrived with one of my comrades in custody. One of them was very agitated and began to beat him up, so using my one good leg I leapt from the grassy bank down on to the detective. Immediately the rest of the detectives jumped into the fray. A general melee ensued for some minutes before one of them shone a light on us all and managed to calm the situation.

My comrade and I were brought to Monaghan Garda station where we were held overnight. I could barely stand – my right thigh was very swollen and painful – and my comrade had blood coming out his ears, so they called a doctor to examine each of us. He came into my cell where I was lying on the bed. He had to cut open my trouser leg up to my right hip to examine the wound in my thigh, as my leg was so swollen. He proclaimed that the leg was not broken and left. And that was it. The wound received no treatment. The next morning we were brought before the court in Monaghan, where we refused to recognise its jurisdiction to try us. We were bloody, bruised and battered. I was limping, and one trouser leg was hanging loose since the doctor had cut it along its length. From the look on his face the judge was not impressed and sentenced each of us to twelve months, the maximum he could impose at that time. We were then taken, under armed escort, to Mountjoy Prison and held overnight in a cell in the basement, to be processed the following morning.

The Chief Prison Officer, who knew me from my previous spell in the prison, became very agitated when he saw me and warned the other jailers to watch me as he said I was 'a right scoundrel'. He was still angry with me because of the hole they found in the wall of the cell I occupied the last time I was there. We were quickly processed and passed into D Wing with the republican prisoners. There were fewer than thirty prisoners in the wing at that time and we were a close-knit community. We had our own exercise yard and also had access, under escort, to the handball alley.

At the end of D Wing was a door which led into the 'hang house' where executions had been carried out. The treble cell next to it was our recreation room. This had formerly been the condemned cell, where McCurtain and other prisoners awaiting execution had been held in isolation except for two jailers being present at all times. This cell had an open fireplace and we negotiated for and were allocated turf for the fire in cold weather.

The prison food at that time was atrocious. Breakfast was a mug of tea in a metal container that would burn your lips if you tried to drink the tea hot, a small loaf of doughy bread baked in the prison, a pat of butter, and porridge if you could stomach it. Prisoners used the porridge as glue to stick pictures on cell walls. Dinners were served on aluminium plates which were stacked on top of each other without dividers, so when one plate was lifted the dinner on the plate below stuck to the bottom of it and had to be scraped off. We got either brown or red meat and we could not distinguish what sort it was either by taste or appearance, likewise the vegetables. Sometimes the two potatoes were edible, and for the year I spent there I never ate a full dinner. Tea was as breakfast, only with jam instead of butter. At that period we were allowed food parcels and that's what sustained us. We pooled our food and cooked on the open fire in the recreation room. We organised our own roster, rotating cooks and fire maintenance. Each morning we would gather in the 'Rec', enjoy our own breakfast and listen to the ten o'clock news on the communal radio.

The injury to my right thigh was causing me serious bother and I could barely walk at times. The surface wound had healed but the muscle was doubled back on itself and was very painful. The prison refused to get me treatment or bring me to the Mater Hospital across the road. After five months of agitation they brought me to St Bricken's, the army hospital on Infirmary Road near the Phoenix Park. I was put in the first bed inside the door, in a big ward with barred windows. It was about half full of soldiers. There were two armed Special Branch detectives positioned in the opposite bed space across the ward from my bed. The other patients were obviously very curious about who I was and what was happening. I was taken for tests and x-rays and was also examined by the army surgeon who, before he saw the x-rays, thought there might be shrapnel in my thigh despite my assuring him otherwise. I was scheduled to be operated on the following morning at 11 a.m.

Later that afternoon my Mum actually got in to visit me, as the prison had notified her where I was. While she was there I went to the toilet and wrote a note to a friend outside and slipped it to my Mum, whispering to her to deliver it that evening. I was trying to set up my escape from the hospital. After she had left, the evening meal was brought around. A little while later a soldier on crutches made his way down to me, 'just for chat', as he told my guards. He asked me what unit I was in and was surprised when I told him I was a political prisoner from Mountjoy. I noticed he reported back to a soldier in a bed about halfway along the ward. He returned and invited me to play Solo with them, so I got up and went to join them, followed by my two Special Branch shadows.

The soldier in the bed was Sergeant Joe Flanagan, who had lost both feet by hand grenade while serving with the United Nations in the Congo. He put me at ease immediately, and I liked him a lot. We played Solo, and yarned and enjoyed ourselves. Joe was open and optimistic despite his injuries, and was very glad he was in the care of the UN doctors because he was to be fitted with artificial feet and would be able to walk again. After a while he opened his locker and offered me a drink. He had whiskey and vodka and beer and he poured me a generous whiskey. Then he asked the two detectives if they would like a drink and when they said yes he quickly retorted, 'Well you better fuck off down to the pub so, because you won't get any here!' When one of them began to remonstrate with him, he ordered them away from his bed and back to the end of the ward, telling them that he was under the protection of the UN and if they annoyed him he would be contacting his UN doctor. They moved away, muttering, while the soldiers grinned with delight. I told him not to get himself into trouble over me, but he just laughed. 'It's not everyday we get an IRA guest in here. Come on, let's enjoy the evening.' And that we did, until the night nurse came on her rounds and discovered me playing cards and drinking whiskey in the early hours. 'And you for operation in the morning!'

A few hours later, a bit fuzzy headed, I was taken to the operating theatre. I came out of the anaesthetic about 6 p.m. that evening and my new soldier friends came to see how I was. We played cards at my bed, and again the poor detectives had to move down the ward away from us.

About noon the next day I was informed that I was to be transferred back to the prison. So much for any possibility of escape! I demanded to see the surgeon who had operated on me, but he told me it was not his choice, that he was under orders to transfer me immediately, by ambulance, 'to the hospital in the prison'. When I told him there was no hospital in the prison he went away 'to see what he could do'. On his return he reiterated that he was under orders 'from the very top' and I would be taken by ambulance to Mountjoy Prison in about an hour. I pointed out that patients did not usually walk into hospital for treatment and be discharged in an ambulance, but rather the reverse. Demanding my clothes, I told him I would refuse to leave in an ambulance and resist any effort to force me. I would walk out of the hospital. 'You can't walk in your condition,' he replied. 'Then I should be kept in hospital,' I told him. Eventually I got my clothes, and one of the soldiers helped me get dressed. They were very upset about what was happening and were glad to lend me a crutch. Some time later more Special Branch arrived, and I hobbled out of the ward to loud farewells from my new soldier friends and the nurses. I got down the stairs with some difficulty, refusing any help from my escort.

There was an ambulance waiting but I refused to get into it. Some of the police wanted to force me in but, aware that soldiers and hospital staff were watching, they decided not to press the issue. Instead, they told me to get into one of the Special Branch escort cars. As I could not bend my right leg, I occupied all of the back seat. I gave back the crutch to a nurse, who smiled sweetly and waved. We then headed in a two-car convoy for the prison.

We drove through the prison gates to the main administration block where the governor, 'Johnny Kavanagh' as we called him, was standing with a cordon of jailers armed with batons. Without a crutch I had to hop on one foot up the steps and lean against the wall at the door where he was waiting. He attacked me verbally and ordered me to the 'hospital wing', a group of cells in C Wing where ordinary prisoners were held if they were ill. I refused to go there, insisting I would return to my own cell in D Wing, to my comrades, who would look after me better than the state would. When he saw my determination to resist if necessary, he relented. I was escorted, hopping on one foot, to D Wing. He refused to allow me crutches. After negotiations with my OC I was given a walking stick. Gradually my leg healed and I was able to walk, run and play handball again.

The state re-introduced the Special Criminal Court as a military court, that is to say, criminal trial by three military officers above the rank of commandant. This is a non-jury court established by the Offences Against the State Act, 1939, for the trial of political offences. It can be introduced at any time by government order. It is usually a tribunal of three members who need not be judges. A number of republicans were arrested and brought before that court and received heavy sentences. They were all put in D Wing, with us. This was clearly the state making a big effort to break the IRA and to put an end to the campaign, such as it was.

One of the ordinary prisoners, whom I later learned was a bit off the head, attempted to stab me one day as I was walking back from the handball alley. I tried to grab his knife wrist and only succeeded in gripping the blade, which I held tightly as I punched him as hard as I could on the jaw. He fell back and scrambled away from me and I discovered that the palm of my left hand had a deep cut across it and was bleeding profusely. I was taken to the prison medic, who bandaged my hand and gave me an anti-tetanus injection.

Seven nights later I woke up in my cell, itching all over and I could not sleep; by morning my joints were all swollen, my eyes were almost closed and my jaws were locked. I had lockjaw, which the injection was supposed to prevent. When I did not show up on the wing after opening time some of my comrades came into my cell and, seeing my condition, sent for medical help. They later told me they thought I had polio or something like that. I was carried to the hospital wing and, fortunately for me, the doctor who examined me knew I'd been given anti-tetanus the week before and could administer the antidote. I was delirious and felt like I was burning up. I do not remember the treatment except that they brought in a large container, like a big bucket, and coated me all over in a kind of grease which cooled down my body. This was done every few hours over two or three days until my temperature returned to normal. As I began to recover, the bed, saturated with the grease, became very uncomfortable. I managed to get to my feet and strip the bed, intending to turn the single mattress, but as I tried to lift it I realised I was too weak and had to call for help. The medical orderly heard me and organised a new mattress and bedding and I was much more comfortable after that. I was shocked that I was so physically weak.

While I was in the hospital wing the OC visited me and told me that the IRA had issued a statement ending the armed campaign. Even though it was inevitable and was achieving nothing towards ending British occupation I remember I was more upset by that news than my predicament. Over the following days lying there alone I had time to reflect upon the campaign and my small part in it. I knew the campaign had been a failure in that we had not achieved our objectives. Right through our history, generation after generation had offered resistance and tried to achieve freedom. Some of those attempts had failed miserably but each of them had, at another level, kept the spirit of freedom alive. I consoled myself with the hope that we had at least achieved that. A few days later I got back to D Wing. The remainder of my sentence was uneventful and, now 23 years old, I was released in March 1962.

6

Prisoners were released about 8 a.m. When my two comrades and I were let out through the gates, we were met by Clarrie and Muriel in a horse-drawn hackney cab. We were driven, chatting and laughing, to an early house for a pint, and then for a good breakfast. We reminisced about our previous experience going through town with Bang Bang chasing after us. Having arranged to meet again that evening, the women went to their respective jobs. I went home to see my folks and enjoyed a few hours with them catching up with each other's news. That afternoon I headed back into town and wandered through the city enjoying my new freedom. In the evening I rejoined my comrades and we spent some time together until we met up with Clarrie and Muriel again. We went for a meal and a few drinks. It was very nice being in good company and pleasant surroundings again.

Clarrie and I started going out together. We dated regularly, and over time our relationship became more serious. Being also in the movement, she understood where I was at politically. And when we spoke of marrying, there was the clear understanding between us that I would continue my activities afterwards. There was little employment in Ireland and times were hard. It was particularly difficult for me, as whenever I managed to land a job, Special Branch would visit my employer 'suggesting' it would be better if I was let go. A number of employers told me about this and apologised for letting me go. Eventually, by the end of the year, I had to emigrate. It was the last thing I wanted to do, but without a job or money I had no choice. I discussed it all with Clarrie. We agreed to keep in touch and be together as soon as we could.

That winter of 1962–63 was a bitter one. I went to London in January 1963 with two friends, Hugh and Bobby, and £1.10 to my name. Fortunately, a pal put us up for a few days until we could find a flat. We were glad to find a place in Shepherds Bush; it was really a large bedsit, with the bathroom down the hall. There had been heavy falls of snow in London and we did not see the actual pavements for nearly six weeks. It was almost impossible to get work and we had a hungry few weeks, existing on onion sandwiches and tea.

The landlady lived alone in the house and took an immediate shine to Bobby, much to his horror and our amusement. She was a buxom woman in her forties and easy on the eye. Bobby, on the other hand, was shy and inexperienced. Neither Hugh nor I would have refused her attentions, especially as we had no money to pay the rent. But all she wanted was Bobby. There was no key on the bathroom door, and if she knew Bobby was in the bath she would go in after him. It got to the point that he would not stay in the house on his own. And he would only use the bath if we were nearby.

Eventually we all got work in Wandsworth, across the city. Hugh got a job as a store man in Philips Electric, while Bobby and I got work in a wire and cable factory operating machines we had never seen before. But we managed it ok. The work was dusty and the pay was poor. But we were glad to have it.

Some weeks later we left that job and started work in the store with Hugh. The wages were better, and it was fun working together. Sometimes I needed to be alone for a while, so at lunchtime I would go walkabout, exploring the district. One fine day, as I sat on a bench on Wandsworth Common doing a crossword in my paper, my attention was drawn to a woman cleaning her windows across from me. She was a good-looking woman, and when she saw me looking at her she waved to me. I waved back in a casual, light-hearted way. It was nice, and friendly, and made me feel good. London can be a lonely, cold place. And people do not generally salute each other like that, especially an attractive woman to a strange man. When she had finished the window and was about to enter her house, she waved to me again and made a gesture offering me a cuppa. I went over to her, and she said, 'Fancy a cuppa tea, love?'

'Thank you very much,' I replied, 'that would be very nice.'

As we entered her house and went into the kitchen I introduced myself. She told me she was Vicki. We chatted as we had our tea and biscuits, and she began to flirt with me, which I enjoyed. I had to return to work as my lunch break was nearly over, but as I left she gave me a hug and invited me to come back for lunch the next day. I returned to work, smiling to myself. I loved Clarrie, but still, it was nice having Vicky interested. And celibacy did not agree with me.

Next day I went back and she had lunch ready. As we ate, I knew there was an unspoken understanding that we would have sex together. She brought me to her bedroom where we quickly undressed and got into bed together. She was bored, and lonely, and looking for a bit of fun, which suited me fine. Our lovemaking was fast and passionate, and very enjoyable. I had already arranged for Hugh to clock me back in at two o'clock. So we had an hour or so together in bed before I had to leave for work. That was on a Thursday. Her husband was a commercial traveller who went on the road on Mondays and returned Fridays. She asked me back, and we settled for the following Tuesday. I opted out on Wednesdays, but went to see her Tuesday and Thursday lunchtimes. It was fun while it lasted. But as she became more possessive, I stopped going to see her.

There were no mobile phones back then, and every few days I would use the public phone to talk with Clarrie. In late spring she came over to London and got a flat in Shepherds Bush near where I stayed. I would have preferred us living together, but she liked to do things the 'proper' way and would not agree to that idea. Her brother Paddy lived in Luton and worked in Vauxhall Motors, the largest company in Luton at the time. So Clarrie and I moved to Luton, but still to separate flats. And we also started work with Vauxhall; Clarrie got a senior secretarial position, while I started in the factory sweeping floors. It was a good number actually, with regular overtime. We could save some money towards getting married and getting a new flat together.

On 1 August 1963 we returned to Dublin and got married. I was twenty-four and Clarrie was three years younger. After a short honeymoon we went back to Luton to our new flat together. Life was good and we socialised with other Dubliners living in Luton. Inevitably this meant getting together in pubs and my drinking increased, not that I noticed it much. Sometimes we would have people to our flat, or visit friends. But as often as not, we met and socialised in pubs. It was the way of Irish emigrants.

When Clarrie became pregnant we applied for work together in pub management and became landlords in the Blacksmith Arms in Luton. Very quickly word got around that the pub was managed by 'Dubs', and many of our customers were Dubliners living and working locally. Business increased, as did my drinking. Sometimes customers would offer a drink. When the bar closed and the place was cleaned up and ready for the next morning, I would 'relax' with a drink or two. Occasionally Clarrie's brother Paddy and a few friends would help with the cleaning up. Afterwards we'd all retire to the back bar or to our kitchen and have a little party.

In January 1965 our beautiful daughter Anna was born. Clarrie actually worked in the bar up to the time she had to go to the hospital. I had to stay and run the pub, but phoned regularly checking on how she was doing. After Anna was born I went to visit them. The nurses kept remarking on how often I had phoned through the night.

Actually, many of our customers had also phoned, pretending they were 'the husband' in order to be given information.

My brother Pat got tired of bar work in Dublin and came over to Luton. At first he worked in Vauxhall before getting a job elsewhere. It was nice having him in Luton, and he came into the Blacksmiths regularly. Pauline was nursing in London and had married. I visited her and her family whenever our free times coincided.

Later that year we contracted to manage a pub in Bedford. We went home to Dublin between jobs for a holiday to show off our beautiful baby. We stayed with Clarrie's parents. There was much 'oohing' and 'aahing' over Anna, who thrived on it all. Having had a taste of being back in Ireland, the prospect of returning to live in England did not appeal to us. Clarrie suggested we should stay in Dublin. We decided I would return alone to work out our notice in the pub in Bedford until a replacement manager was found. I managed the pub alone for over two months. It was lonely for me being away from Clarrie and Anna.

The public bar was frequented by a tough bunch and had a bad reputation. A friend in Luton loaned me a black German shepherd named Prince that had been police trained. The hard cases feared him. With him by my side, I was able to bar the heavies and make the pub more sociable. On one occasion, after I had barred one of the toughs his cronies tried to set me up for a 'hiding' or worse. One of them hit another customer. I came out from behind the bar to sort it out. When I intervened, the tough swung at my head with his pint glass. As I feinted and clocked him, I felt a pull on my left shoulder as another thug grabbed me from behind. Prince leapt clear over the counter, landing on his shoulders, knocking him to the floor with his jaws locked on his neck. The poor man peed himself in terror. I called Prince to heel and threw the thugs out. After that we had no more trouble in the bar.

With the absence of thugs and hard cases, the clientele changed; decent people began to frequent the pub. At lunchtime, office workers came for coffee and a sandwich, and shoppers began to drop in too. There was the front bar, a middle snug and a large lounge bar at the rear. Two women friends, Annie and Jo, came in regularly at lunchtime for a beer or coffee and a chat. They were happy people who enjoyed their interlude in the snug. One lunchtime, Annie left early to catch a bus, and Jo was still there at the 2 p.m. closing time. When I closed up shop I joined her for a coffee. As I was showing her to the door, we were suddenly hugging and kissing. And, almost without thinking about it, we were upstairs, naked in bed together. And that is where we spent most of the afternoon until just before 5 p.m. when I had to reopen the pub for the evening.

Jo had her own business in town and could sometimes take an hour or so off. When that happened we would go for a walk along the river with Prince, or go to bed. Jo was worldly, undemanding, independent and well off. I liked her a lot, especially as she was very good company. She hoped that I would move in with her and we would live together. But she knew that I was married and had a baby daughter, and understood when I told her that I loved my family and wanted to be with them.

Most evenings a little man came in for a pint as he waited for his bus home from work. He was pleasant, and I enjoyed serving him. Sometimes he'd buy a half ounce of tobacco. One evening he ordered his pint and tobacco and asked me if he could have the items on credit as he had forgotten his wallet. I served him, wondering to myself if I would see him again. He did not come in the next day. But the day after, he did come. He ordered his pint, paid me in full, and thanked me for trusting him. After a few minutes he asked me if I backed the horses. When I said 'Sometimes', he told me to bet on two horses the following day. I forgot about his tips until he came in the next day. He told me the two had won. Over the next month, he tipped me fifteen horses. Thirteen were winners, one was placed and one lost. Apparently he was an accountant with a brother in the horse racing world. When he got tips from his brother he passed them on to me because I had trusted him. I did not gamble big, but I made a nice few pounds while I knew him.

When the bar closed and the day's work was done, I would sometimes like to go for a drink, not even considering the drinks I might have had during the working day as 'drinking'. I would either go to another pub for 'afters', or some other pub managers would come to my place. Quite often I would not get to bed until the early hours. As far as I was concerned it was social drinking and seemed to have no adverse effect on me. I had a huge capacity for drink.

When a new manager was appointed I returned home to Dublin to live with Clarrie at her parents' place. I liked Clarrie's parents, especially her mother whom I fondly called Mrs Mac. Clarrie was already employed as a secretary nearby, with her mother watching Anna during the day. I got a job selling vacuum cleaners and floor polishers with Electrolux. My sales area was the south-west suburbs of the city. I bought a cheap used car and was in business. I was allocated a door-to-door canvasser, and when she got orders I demonstrated the machine and tried to make a sale. I was surprised to see how lonely many of the women were. Quite often they would express an interest in buying a machine just to break up the monotony of their lives, and/or to check out the salesman for a bit of excitement. One woman made an advance on me. I told her I was married and not interested, which she accepted gracefully. The following week I was called to a house in a neighbouring road and something similar happened. Then about a week or so later in the same neighbourhood a different woman tried the same approach. Accepting failure, she invited me to have a coffee, over which she laughingly told me that she was sister to the first woman and a friend to the second. The three of them had decided that each one would try to seduce me, and had bet against each other. In their individual and collective boredom with their suburban lives they had sought to generate a little excitement.

While this was the only such concentrated instance, it was not unusual, while demonstrating machines, that a lonely woman would attempt intimacy with me. I learned that other salesmen had similar experiences. Some were very attractive – and I was tempted. But I did not want to complicate my life any more than it was already. Living with in-laws was difficult. Clarrie's parents were very nice people, but the intimacy necessary in a marriage was next to impossible in the crowded conditions.

I reconnected with the IRA, in so far as that was possible in my situation. It was a period of re-building the organisation and moving it towards a socialist perspective, with which I agreed. Sometimes, rather than sit at home with my in-laws I would go to a local pub in the village. The first evening, I went there about 10 p.m. Closing time was 11 p.m. I went in to the back bar, where some men were playing darts. I was greeted cordially enough, and Peter, the publican, served me. He was a great old man. He wore his hat behind the bar, as well as a black apron. I was surprised that the bar emptied five minutes before closing time. I assumed that as it was Wednesday, maybe the guys were simply short of money. I drank up, said good night to Mr Harte and strolled back home. The following Sunday I went back at lunchtime and met my old friend Paddy Ennis, who I discovered was a regular. I joined his company. He went to the toilet, and came back chortling gleefully with what he had been told while out. The reason the bar emptied before closing time on Wednesday was because the regulars thought that I, being tall, clean shaven and tidy, was a Garda checking on after-hours drinking! We all had a good laugh and business returned to normal.

I realised that hard selling was not for me, and after a couple of months I left that job. I got work as despatch supervisor in Richmond Foods, about twenty minutes' drive from home in County Kildare. They produced sausages and cooked meat products. After a few months the production manager left and I was given his job. I had a staff of over one hundred, mostly women. I enjoyed the challenge of doing something new and it went well. I had to estimate production requirements in the morning and set things going. Then, when the orders had all come in I would know how good my estimate had been and if necessary adjust production. It was like a guessing game each day. I enjoyed the work and, as soon as we had enough money, Clarrie and I moved into a rented house on our own.

There was a young lad named Timmy working in the factory. He was small and very thin. He was so slight that the smallest white coat reached to his ankles and he'd have to roll the sleeves up. Even the smallest white cap was too large for him and sat on his ears. It was his job to hose down the production area during the general lunch break. He took a later lunch. I gave him little thought until one day, as I came up the back stairway after my lunch, I came upon him sitting on the stairs crying. I sat beside him and asked what was wrong. Between sobs, he told me that he was hungry. He had no money to buy his lunch and had not eaten all day. I sent him to the canteen with the price of a lunch. When I got to my office I called the canteen supervisor and asked her to see that Timmy was well fed. Then I called Elsie, the floor supervisor, in to my office and she told me about Timmy. Apparently he had a step-mother who treated him very badly. He had to bring her his wages, unopened. And quite often she would 'forget' to give him his lunch money or would hold back his allowance. The poor wee fella was working hard and not getting enough to eat. Sometimes he got no dinner when he got home either.

I went to my boss and told him the story. I suggested that Timmy's overtime be paid to him separate to his basic wage, so he would at least have some earnings for himself. And my boss agreed. Timmy was delighted with this arrangement. Each pay day he would receive his wage packet and then go to the office to be given his overtime in a separate envelope. I explained to him that the overtime was his, to do with as he wished. I told him not to tell anyone at home about it. After a few months of eating well, and with no worries, Timmy began to fill out, showing the benefits of the nourishment. He became a really happy person about the factory.

During the following Christmas week I hurried back one day from lunch to plan the afternoon production schedule. The workers seemed to be watching me more than usual, but I quickly put that out of my mind. I noticed that the factory floor was not as clean as it could be. Spotting Jimmy, I called him to me and gave out to him about it as I headed to my office. Elsie came in with me. When I went to my desk to consult my production ledger there was a brown paper bag sitting on top of it. I became furious, and angrily swept the paper bag off my desk onto the floor, muttering about people cluttering up my work space. Elsie picked up the paper bag and put it back on my desk. In a quiet, firm voice she told me I should open it. I was about to explode again, but something in her expression stopped me. I opened the bag to find a Christmas card and a box of handkerchiefs, from Timmy. His card read, 'Happy Christmas, Mr Pringle. Thank you for everything.' I think I must have gone into shock momentarily. I was deeply touched, and ashamed and tearful. Elsie was smiling broadly. And when I looked out to the factory everyone there, except Timmy, was watching me. I took a deep breath, went out to Timmy and apologised. I thanked him. We gave each other a big hug and all the workers applauded. What a day! It was an experience I shall never forget.

One day, passing through the cold store area, I came on a crisis situation. A worker was locked in a cold room and the lock was jammed. A fitter was pulling on the door handle and asked me for help. At minus 40 degrees Celsius he had to be released immediately. I reached over and we gave a mighty tug together. The door jerked open and the worker staggered out. But I had pulled a muscle in my back. I was off work for several days, in severe pain and barely able to move. But I recovered well.

It was 1967, and I had been in the factory two years. While I enjoyed the work, it did not pay very well, so Clarrie continued watching the newspaper adverts for a better job for me. I think she hoped to improve our lives by improving my employment prospects. Prompted by her, I applied for, and got, a job managing a small bakery in County Tipperary. I went ahead, to rent a house and start work. She was pregnant again and stayed with her parents until the baby was born. It was a boy this time. Thomas was a fine healthy baby and another delight in our lives. After she came out of hospital I collected my family and brought them to join me in Tipperary. The work was interesting, for a while. But gradually it became routine and monotonous. I missed the hustle and bustle of the factory and the daily challenges while working there. If there is no challenge or variety in doing something, it becomes very monotonous to me.

We visited my family in Dublin occasionally and I enjoyed the odd pint with my Dad. But then my Mum became ill with cancer. She was very strong-willed and self-sufficient, and had no time for fussing about. When she got the cancer she did not go to the doctor until she had to, but by then it was too late. When the hospital could do no more for her, rather than go to a hospice she went in to a nursing home in Rathgar. This was her favourite part of the city, and not far from where my parents lived. Dad knew and respected what she wanted, and made the necessary bookings.

Visiting her and sitting with her, I knew she would soon leave us. She knew this too. And in her typical style she accepted it and would not make a fuss about it. She maintained her dignity right to the end, insisting on going to the bathroom rather than use a bed pan. Eyes still sparkling and her spirit strong, she would ask me to walk with her. And she'd hold on to my arm for support as she shuffled to the bathroom. It was shocking seeing how physically frail she had become, although her spirit was strong. Heartbroken, I'd wait for her and escort her back to her bed. She passed away quietly, my Dad by her side. Pauline and Pat were home, and being all together eased our pain and grief. Again I met aunts and uncles, cousins, nieces and nephews. Weddings and funerals seem to be the only occasions when I see my relations. That evening I walked alone for hours, as I just could not be in company at the time.

7

y work in the bakery was mostly administration, with forays out on the road to find new customers. I had use of a company car. We had three bread van routes, and if one of our salesmen was off work I would do his rounds. As well as bread, there was a fine confectionery section; the selection of pastries was mouth-watering. What with too much sitting and pastry sampling, my weight and girth increased. I had to start a strict regime of exercise and dieting to control my weight. I began walking again.

On the surface everything was fine – but something was happening within me that I did not understand. I cannot rationally explain, even to myself, except to relate how I felt and what happened. Clarrie encouraged me to join the local Junior Chamber of Commerce, which I reluctantly did. The members were nice people and sociable, but their focus of interest was anathema to me. My outlook was socialist and republican. My sympathy was with the working class. I had no respect for big business, or the ambitions of the members. I was like a fish out of water. I also felt I was being compared to my in-laws who were, as they say, doing very well for themselves. My drinking increased and I only felt comfortable in the pub.

A year later our beautiful second daughter Lulu was born, which brought me out of my doldrums for a while. I was married to a lovely woman and we had three wonderful children. I had a job and a company car. I was in the Junior Chamber and the future should have looked good. But I was barely functioning, at work or at home. I was also less active in the movement, which had deviated from armed struggle towards socialism and social agitation. And this was focused mainly in the cities, away from where I lived. I agreed with the move to the Left, and the general direction the movement was going. I was less easy with the idea that the IRA should give up any idea of armed struggle in the future. I argued, unsuccessfully, for the retention of a core group, or groups, within the IRA to be trained and available as needs might arise.

I hardly noticed that I was drinking more and more. Beer was being replaced by whiskey. I began to take refuge in booze, and with other 'boozers', finding fault with almost everything in my life, ever feeling more boxed in and frustrated. Within myself I was filled with desperation and out of place in my world. I felt totally alone, even when I was in company.

It cannot have been easy for Clarrie either, being stuck at home all the time. She had been used to having a job; now her only job was at home with the children. At weekends we went on outings with the children to the mountains or to one of the lakes. These trips were pleasant and enjoyable; the children were wonderful. Sometimes we went to Dublin to visit Clarrie's parents at the weekends. I had little in common with her family and I began to resent having to make those trips. Again I took refuge in the pub, which did not help matters.

While driving Clarrie's mother back to Dublin one day we gave a lift to two Canadian hitch-hikers. Mrs Mac chatted with them most of the way. They were going to stay in a hostel in the city centre. She suggested I drop her off first and then bring the hitch-hikers into the city. I did this, and then went for a drink with them in Dublin. We exchanged information and parted. A week or so later one of them phoned me at work. She was going to Limerick. On impulse I arranged to meet her there. She seemed like a breath of fresh air to me in my doldrums. We began an affair, which went on over a few weeks, until she left for London to find work.

I became even more down in myself. My only relief seemed to be in booze. I was unable to retrieve my home life, which was tense and unhappy for us all. I felt totally useless. Ready to explode inside, I had to get away. In despair and desperation I told Clarrie I was leaving. I gave up my job. This was all totally irrational and very hurtful to Clarrie and my family. I cannot excuse myself or perhaps even explain myself properly, except to say that I could do nothing else at the time.

Broken-hearted, I left and went to London, not realising or even considering that my family might be devastated by my actions. I reconnected with the two Canadian women in London, and we shared a flat in Brixton. I got a job on a building site, and then a part-time job window cleaning three mornings a week before I went to the building site. Each morning on my way to work I passed a school and saw children being dropped off by their mothers or fathers. Sometimes a little girl or boy would look forlornly after their parent. That 'look' struck me to my core. Filled with pain and grief, the image of those little children stayed with me. They became my children, in my mind's eye. I was tortured within myself. Clarrie and I wrote to each other. And after a few months I asked if I could come home. And she agreed.

Returning home, jobless and penniless, I tried to put my life back together again with my family. I got a job in a grain mill for a while. I managed to buy a cheap car and an industrial vacuum cleaner and started to work for myself, cleaning chimneys. Not the cleanest or best paid job in the world, but at least I was working for myself and my family. It was a struggle to make a decent living, but the struggle within myself was much greater. I was filled with shame and remorse – and great sorrow. I was not drinking, and I could not see that drink had been any part of my problems.

Around this time the Northern Ireland Civil Rights Association (NICRA) was actively campaigning for equality in the North, seeking the right to vote for nationalist people there. The savage reaction of the RUC, B Specials and Orange Order to peaceful demonstrations and to the possible rise of the nationalist population created a volatile situation. Once the IRA took up an armed defence and the gun entered into the equation, the people went off the streets. The peaceful movement towards expression of civil rights through NICRA was stymied. Whole streets in nationalist areas of Belfast and Derry were burnt out. People began fleeing across the border into the South, creating Irish refugees in Ireland.

The views held by the leadership in the 1960s, that the possibility of armed struggle was over, resulting in the decision not to re-build in that direction, meant that the IRA was not adequately prepared to defend the nationalist people in the North when they came under attack. The rise of NICRA, and the move by nationalists for civil rights in the North, was supported by republicans. But the leadership was left behind, not able to read the political significance of that spontaneous surge towards civil rights and the basic demand for 'one man, one vote'. The nationalist people in the North were leading the way, leaving the IRA behind.

The inadequacy of the IRA in the face of the attacks against the nationalists in the North, together with the move away from the policy of abstention in elections, formed the catalyst for the Right-wing elements within the republican movement to engineer a major split. Thus, the Provisional IRA and Provisional Sinn Féin were established. They became known as the Provos. They had argued, with conviction, that the leadership had failed the nationalist people in the North. But I knew the people on both sides of the division and could not bring myself to support the Right-wing elements, or a split. While I agreed that the IRA leadership had failed the people, I felt that a split would not solve the problems and I could not align myself with the Right-wing elements. I remained with the original movement, which became known as the Official IRA and Official Sinn Féin. I became active again, as far as I was able in my home situation, mostly gathering up whatever useful materials were available locally and getting them to the North.

Again, Clarrie spotted an advert for a better position. This time it was for a development manager in the co-operative movement in Glencolmcille, south-west Donegal. With her encouragement and her tuition in Irish – a requirement of the job – I applied for the position. Having passed the first two interviews, I had my final one attended by Fr McDyer, the founder and president of the co-operatives. I landed the position. He organised a house for us to rent in the parish, so we loaded up our belongings and set off for Donegal.

Fr McDyer introduced me to the various co-ops and the people involved. I began to realise the challenge ahead of me and relished the opportunity to try solving the various problems. There were six enterprises in the group. I was to oversee a hand-knitting co-op, a holiday village, a folk village, a small silversmiths and a building co-op. There was also a knitwear factory with a professional manager, which did not need me. My most urgent and immediate task was to try to salvage the building co-op, which employed over twenty men.

The reverend was a great innovator, but had little skill at running a business. His concept of a co-operative society seemed to mean that he would be the boss, which was understandable given his clerical position and sense of hierarchy. We clashed quite often on the issue, until I let it drop and focused all my concentration on sorting out the building co-op. This enterprise had built the holiday village and the folk village. And it had already started on a ten-house development for the county council when I arrived on the scene.

My research into the building co-op revealed that it had not been fully paid for its construction of the holiday village. To my surprise, the holiday village was not a co-op but a private business, although it was portrayed as a co-op. After lengthy and tough negotiations, the holiday village company paid an agreed balance to the building co-op, which helped enormously.

I liked my new job very much. The school bus collected the children from home, and brought them back again in the afternoon. I was able to go home most days for lunch. Clarrie seemed to be very happy. We were closer with each other again, which was very nice. She was busy with a variety of craft projects with local women. And I was busy, once again, in a challenging job interacting with many people. We lived in a beautiful area, with lots of beaches within easy reach. There were lovely glens and hills, and the children really enjoyed going on outings. Anna was reading before she was 3 years old and loved books, and Thomas and Lulu also grew to love them. With visitors coming to our house from all walks of life, and politics being a regular topic of conversation, they grew up articulate and interested in worldly matters.

On one occasion Anna was sitting doing nothing and I asked was anything the matter. She replied, 'I'm just bored.'

'You don't want to go outside and play?' I asked.

'No. Do you know what I'd love to do?'

'Tell me.'

'I'd love to run away.'

'To run away? Well, why don't you?' I said this knowing that there was nowhere to run to from our house, as we were 3 miles from Glencolmcille.

Some time later my family spent a week visiting Clarrie's parents, while I continued working. The following Sunday morning I arrived to bring them back to Donegal. When I entered their house, I knew immediately that something was amiss. The tension was obvious. Almost in tandem, Clarrie and her father told me that I would have to deal with Anna. When the story unfolded, I was told that Anna had been staying a few nights at her aunt Ann's. Early on Saturday morning she coaxed her cousins Paula and Rhona to run away with her. But for Uncle Richard searching and finding them, God knows what might have happened. Anna was now barred from ever staying with them again. Richard had punished his young daughters. And now I was expected to punish Anna.

I could see Anna watching me apprehensively. And everyone else was waiting for me to take action. First I had a cup of tea, just to give myself a chance to consider the situation. Then I took Anna by the hand and said, 'We are going for a walk in the park, to sort this out.' Anna and I walked into the park nearby. And when we were out of sight and alone, we sat on a bench. Turning to her, I asked, 'Why did you run away?'

'Sure, you told me to. Remember that time back home?' she replied.

The plan had been that she and Paula would get up early, get the bus into Dublin, buy presents for everyone, and then go to Cafolla's Café in O'Connell Street and get knickerbocker glories. These were big ice creams, in a tall glass with fruit and juice. The children loved them. Then they planned to go to a movie and be back home by early evening. The first hitch came when Paula's younger sister Rhona woke up and insisted on going too. The end came when Uncle Richard caught up with them as they waited for the bus to the city. Apparently, when Richard and Aunt Ann woke up and could not hear the children, Richard went to check on them and discovered they were missing. He immediately went searching for them, and they were caught.

When Anna's story unfolded, I felt so proud of her. I was also amused by her account. Little did I think that weeks earlier, when I had asked her why she hadn't away, that she would actually try to do so. Now I was expected to punish her, for what I had done myself when I was a child. I told her of my escapade when I was 4 years old. And we laughed together as we sat on the park bench. As far as I was concerned punishment was out of the question. I told her to leave everything to me but to promise to keep our own counsel. She was to look solemn, and whatever she did, not to laugh when we got back to Granny's house. When we entered the living room they all looked up in expectation of some explanation from me about Anna's punishment. I simply said, 'Anna is very sorry about what she did. I have dealt with her. And that is the end of the matter. Let us all leave it at that.' During lunch I could not catch Anna's eye lest we might both start laughing. We returned home to Donegal that evening.

Being based in Donegal I was now close to Derry. This made it easier to be supportive of the Official IRA there. The Bogside and Creggan areas had been barricaded off, and Crown forces had no access to them. Entry to 'Free Derry' was by a circuitous route, through a maze of narrow back lanes. On one occasion, driving into Derry with some materials, I was stopped at a British Army checkpoint. It had just been set up. There were half a dozen cars already lined up, waiting to be searched. I had no possibility of making a u-turn, so I had to sit and await the inevitable. When my turn came to be searched, I produced my driving licence to one soldier while another opened the front passenger door. A third soldier began to slide the mirror on a trolley under my car to inspect it. Clarrie had been collecting Green Shield Stamps, and there were sheets of them in the glove compartment and strewn on the floor under the front passenger seat. The soldier got all excited, calling to his comrade. 'Hey Bert, look at all the Green Shield Stamps!' He held some up for Bert to see. When I asked why the interest in the stamps, he told me they were collecting them to help some children in an orphanage. Bert had called the soldier with the mirror, and now the three of them were looking in on me and the Green Shield Stamps.

'Do you want them? My missus collects them. There are books of them at home. You can have these if they'll help some children. Go on, take them. You're welcome.'

'Oh good,' he said as he gathered up the stamps, stuffing them inside his jacket. 'Thanks, mate!'

With that my licence was returned, the mirror retrieved and I was waved through the checkpoint to everyone's satisfaction – mine most of all.

One morning as we had our coffees we noticed that Lulu was acting strange, almost as if she were drunk. We discovered she had an empty container for travel sickness tablets, and realised she had eaten a lot of the tablets, which were like sweets to her. We quickly got her into the car and drove into Glencolmcille to the doctor's house, making sure that she would not fall asleep on the way. Dr de Vere was a wonderful physician, and we were blessed that he was at home and knew what to do. He instructed his wife to make lots of sweet tea while he examined Lulu, who was in my arms as I sat on a chair. Rather than pump out the little one's tummy, which can be quite traumatic for a child, he fed her the tea until she threw up. And we kept doing that for hours until he decided that she was clear. We were with him from about 11 a.m. until 5 p.m. As Lulu went through her ordeal, she ranted and raved and gripped my beard with amazing strength as I held her to me. Eventually she calmed down and rested on my lap.

The doctor told us to take her home and let her rest. He said she would wake in about three hours. She would be hyperactive afterwards, but not to be disturbed by that. That evening he called to our house to give her a gentle sedative, saying she would sleep all night and not remember a thing in the morning. Our great neighbours looked after Anna and Thomas when they came home from school. Lulu experienced no after-effects, thanks to the good doctor's care.

Everything went along fine with my job, until an article was published in *The Irish Times* about Glencolmcille and the co-ops there. It stated that 'Peter Pringle, a former internee, was Development Manager in the Co-ops'. As a result, the Special Branch raided my house and my office while I was away on co-op business. My office was in a building which also contained a supermarket, bakery and confectionery. There was nothing to be found, of course.

But they said they got the smell of gelignite in or about my office. The only thing they could have smelled was the marzipan used in the confectionery next door. Interestingly, marzipan can smell similar to gelignite. Ironically, the *Irish Times* article was written by Seán Cronin, who formerly had himself been a senior IRA figure and was also interned in The Curragh when I was there.

Some time later, Fr McDyer sent for me. He showed me a letter he had received from his bishop, stating that it was improper to have a person such as me managing the co-ops. Part of my salary was made up of a grant from the government, and I was told this would be withdrawn if I remained as development manager. I was a year working there at this stage, and had not ever received my full salary because the reverend maintained the government grant had not yet come through.

To complicate matters, Clarrie was pregnant with our youngest son, John. But she was great, and accepted the situation with courage. In the interest of the co-ops, and after discussing it all with Clarrie, I handed in my notice, on condition that I would immediately receive the back pay due to me. Yet I was not paid my overdue salary until I voiced my intention to go public and expose matters.

The only employment prospect open to me was to try to get work on one of the trawlers fishing out of Killybegs. I got a berth with Sonny Daly on the *Nordhavid*, a Swedish-built 70-footer. The boat was then based in Dún Laoghaire, on the east coast, and I started fishing there. This meant I had to be away from home again, but that could not be helped. At first I got seasick. But I loved the work and being at sea, and so I persisted with it.

There was a Lancashire man named Davy on the boat when I joined her. He observed me going to the stern getting sick and called me into the galley. He made a cheese sandwich (a 'cheese butty' he called it) and insisted I eat it, telling me that this was the way to beat seasickness. After a few bites I was throwing up over the rail again. When I returned to the galley he insisted I eat some more. Sure enough, after a while my stomach settled. When the boat tied up for the weekend Davy would go to the pub 'to sup a few beers', as he put it. He would spend Friday night, all day Saturday and Sunday supping beer, until the boat sailed at midnight Sunday. Nobody dared speak to him on Monday. On Tuesday he would grunt a reply, and by Wednesday he would be normal again. He was a quiet man, and I never heard him say a bad word about anyone.

Davy was amazing in that he seemed to be able to communicate with the seagulls. They would land on the rail beside him when he was gutting fish, and take offerings from his hand as he talked softly to them. When a shot of fish was on deck the gulls would fly down in large numbers to grab some. The crew would yell at them, waving their arms to scare them away. If Davy was on deck he would quietly speak to the gulls, 'Go on now. We'll feed you later.' And they would rise away from the fish while he was on deck. If the catch was small it wouldn't take a flock of gulls long to deplete it. Where the fish were on deck it was sectioned off and boarded up in pounds so that the fish would not be scattered about the deck as the boat rolled. When a gull landed in a pound to take a fish it was easy to catch one, as the pounds were only about 4 or 5 feet square. Sometimes a deckhand would catch a gull and cross its wings so it could not fly and leave it sitting among the fish. The other gulls would not risk coming low, seeing its distress. I much preferred the method Davy showed me. This was to catch a gull and, holding it between my hands, rock it gently to sleep and put it down, still sleeping, among the fish, which had the same effect on the other gulls. After working the boat in the Irish Sea for a few weeks, we brought her around the north coast to Killybegs.

In June of that year our son John was born. He was a fine strapping lad and brightened up all our lives. Although I was away from home a lot, life was good and Clarrie and the children loved Donegal. There were lots of other children where we lived, and everyone enjoyed themselves.

Life took on a routine. We'd sail from Killybegs about midnight Sunday, landing our catch Tuesday evening. We would sail again at midnight, and land on Thursday evening. On Fridays we had to work about the boat, mending gear, cleaning, taking ice aboard and whatever other jobs might need doing. We usually had Saturdays and Sundays free until the midnight sailing.

One seldom starts off fishing on a high-earning boat. And so it was for me too. As I learned my new trade I also learned what constitutes a good (high-earning) boat. There are five basic conditions necessary to being a successful trawler: a good boat, good gear, a good skipper, a good crew and good luck. If one of those elements is missing it can be difficult; if more than one is missing it is not possible to get big catches and high earnings.

Fishing is hard work. And, ironically, it is harder when fish are scarce than when catches are good. Perhaps this is because there is a joy in a good haul of fish, even with the work of gutting, cleaning, boxing and icing them in the hold. When there is a poor catch the skipper tends to blame the gear, and has the crew adjusting the net, the bridles, the trawl doors, or whatever he thinks might be the problem. Sometimes he will steam to another part of the fishing grounds, taking his worry and frustration out on the crew. It was said that was why the Spanish boats had a small dog aboard. The skipper blamed the mate. The mate blamed the bosun, who blamed the deckhands. They blamed the cook and he blamed the dog, who hid under the galley table until the storm blew over.

8

Clarrie and I became friends with Milton Lesnik and his wife Jean, two Americans who were living in Inver, not far from Killybegs. Milt was a lifelong communist and Trotskyist. He was also a professor of education, and was very interesting and knowledgeable. He had known Trotsky, and had even been in Mexico with him. His sons Peter and Richard became friends too, and Peter fished with us on the *Nordhavid* for some time. We did not earn much, but we had fun as I learned my new trade.

On Sunday 30 January 1972 British Army paratroopers opened fire on peaceful civil rights marchers in Derry, killing thirteen innocent people. The whole country was shocked by the terrible news, and forever more it was known as 'Bloody Sunday'. The following Wednesday, a day of national mourning, I had to drive Milt to Dublin. He was elderly and suffered from vertigo. He may have been frail in body but spiritually and intellectually he was a tower of strength. As we drove through the suburbs into Dublin we saw workers leaving factories and marching spontaneously towards the city centre. We learned that they were going to protest at the British embassy in Merrion Square.

Opting to first call into the Official Sinn Féin offices, I found a leadership meeting in progress. They were trying to decide what action to take to motivate the people after Bloody Sunday. They were surprised when I told them the people were already on the streets in protest and marching on the British embassy. The people had taken the initiative, while the 'revolutionaries' procrastinated.

I managed to park the car not far from Merrion Square, and Milt and I made our way to join the protest. The whole of the east side of the square, where the British embassy was situated, was thronged with angry, mourning people. It was estimated that 20,000 to 30,000 protesters were there. As twilight came, the embassy was attacked with petrol bombs and caught fire, to cheers from the crowd, who prevented the fire brigade getting through to deal with the inferno. The Gardaí were there in force, and baton-charged the crowd, some of whom reacted by throwing stones and whatever came to hand at the Gardaí. In the surging to and fro of the crowd I had some difficulty protecting Milt. I kept him behind me, telling him not to let go of my jacket and to stay close to me. At one level I was exhilarated that the embassy was burning, and so proud that Dublin had arisen in support of the civil rights marchers in Derry. At the same time I was anxiously trying to protect Milt in the middle of the rioting. During one baton-charge I pulled him to one side, standing in front of him, warding off baton blows with my arms. The Gardaí surged past us and we managed to get outside the area of direct hostilities. We left the scene and made it back to the car, relieved to be safe and glad to have been there on that historic occasion.

I had become disillusioned with the Official IRA and ceased to be active with them. I felt their campaign was going nowhere. In May they called a ceasefire, terminating their armed campaign against Crown forces. Then at the end of July, British Army armoured vehicles crashed through the barricades, putting an end to the no-go areas in Derry. All that remained of 'Free Derry' was the slogan painted on a gable wall in the Bogside. But the people were not defeated and the struggle continued.

We were allocated a council house in Killybegs, and we soon adjusted to the move. There were always lots of children playing in and around our house. Thomas looked out for Lulu and John, making sure they were alright. He and Anna were great in that regard. I was not drinking much during this period; my life centred on my family and fishing. Sometimes we would drive to Dublin on Friday evenings, when Clarrie wanted to visit her family. On Saturday mornings Mrs Mac walked up to Ballyfermot to do her shopping. The hill was steep, and it was not easy for the old lady. But she believed she got better bargains there. When we were visiting I would always drive her to the shops, wait for her, and bring her home again. 'Shopping in style,' she called it. I was very fond of her. I often drove back home from Dublin on Sunday evening, and then to the boat to go out fishing at midnight, which could be quite exhausting. Old comrades might visit and sometimes stay with us. And there were many political discussions in our house.

If some incident happened in the west of Ireland the Special Branch would check up on me. If I was at sea at the time they would just enquire about me at home or on the pier, and if I was ashore they might arrest me and detain me for up to forty-eight hours. I understood their policy; and my own policy was to say nothing, except give them my name, address and date of birth. I would sit staring at a wall while they interrogated me over something I knew nothing about. My Dad had advised me: 'If you are ever arrested by that crowd in the Castle, say absolutely nothing, except to give them your name, address and date of birth. No matter what you say, they will twist your words to mean something else.' He was referring to Special Branch, which was based in Dublin Castle.

After my Mum passed away, Dad moved to a small flat in the same street where I was born, though not the same house. Although he was retired and could live on his pension, he went on working. He worked nights, doing security in the Volkswagen building on the Naas Road. He was very fit and walked to and from his work, unless the weather was bad. He loved horse racing, and going to Cheltenham was the highlight of his year. He wasn't a heavy gambler, but knew horses. He had worked with horses as a young man. I often invited him to come stay with us in Donegal, but he thought it was too distant from his chosen lifestyle and so declined my invitations. On one occasion I was a bit insistent in my inviting him for Christmas, telling him I did not want him to be alone. He looked at me with a twinkle in his eye and said, 'What makes you think I'll be alone?', before revealing that he had a woman friend with whom he would spend Christmas and he would bring her to Leopardstown Races on St Stephen's Day. He laughed at the surprise on my face, delighted with his revelation. Not bad for a man of eighty.

One day I received news that he had passed away in his flat. I drove to Dublin and to the city morgue, where I had to identify him. He had come home from work in the morning, had breakfast and a sleep before heading out to do his shopping. He bought a newspaper and studied form over a pint in the local pub. He picked a couple of horses, placed his bets and returned home to make his dinner. After dinner he washed the dishes, lay down for another nap and never woke up. He wasn't missed for two days. A young woman in a neighbouring flat became anxious about not seeing him, and he was discovered dead in his flat.

He lived his life quietly, and he passed away quietly. He was buried alongside my Mum. I met his woman friend, a very nice lady, at his funeral. Afterwards there was a gathering in his brother's house. And this time it was somehow comforting being with all our relations, even though I seldom saw them otherwise.

After some time, and changing from one boat to another, I went fishing on the *Septemar*. She was a 65-foot Irish-built trawler. During the winter months, actually from about September to March or April, we fished herring and mackerel. This was mid-water trawling, two boats fishing in partnership. I loved this fishing most of all, even though the hours were longer than the white fishing. We would sail about 2 p.m. Sunday and work until the following Saturday morning, weather permitting. We might land three or four times during the week, depending on how good the fishing was, and the weather of course.

During the winter period we followed the herring wherever they took us. We could sail out from Killybegs and, finding no fish in Donegal Bay, head on south. Then we would land our catch in Galway and continue working out of there as long as the fishing was good. Sometimes we would be tied up in Galway due to stormy weather. It didn't take us long to find the pubs, where there was music and 'craic'. I love traditional Irish music, and Galway is a great place for music sessions. There were often parties, sometimes on our boat, and my drinking increased accordingly. It seemed to me that there was a continuous party going on in Galway. When we were heading in to land our catch, I would feel an excitement in myself when we had passed the Marguerite buoy, a navigation marker on the way.

When the herring fishing slackened off we would either sail back to Killybegs or go on south to Dunmore East in Waterford, joining the already large fleet of boats fishing from there. At weekends we would lie in Dunmore, or if the weather was bad we would go up the river to Waterford. Usually, when we left Dunmore East for our home port of Killybegs we would go up the west coast, but one year, because of bad weather, we went around to the east. As we were passing Carlingford, steaming around the north coast, we were intercepted and boarded by the British Navy. After searching the boat a young officer came into the galley where our crew were held. He asked me my name and address, which I gave him. When he asked the other crew members, each gave the same address as I had given.

'You all live at the same address?'

'That's right,' we replied. 'We fish together and we live together.'

He shrugged his shoulders. They left our boat and we went on our way to Killybegs without further incident.

Fishermen were paid on the basis of a share of the catch, which meant that if the fishing was poor, or we could not fish due to stormy weather, we received no wages. We could sign on the labour exchange at such times, which helped a little. If the fishing was good then we earned very well. One winter of severe gales we did not fish for almost six weeks and were dependent on the labour exchange. Clarrie was worried, with Christmas looming ever closer. But the gales eased two weeks before Christmas and we got out to fish. We filled the two boats twice in a week and we were fine for Christmas. I suppose that was part of the excitement of herring fishing – hard times with always the possibility of big catches. It was also great to be in a crew which worked well together. It is said that there are no passengers on a trawler. And that was the truth.

During the summer, tourists would come down the pier to watch us land our catch. People often asked for 'a feed of fish', and we would oblige. Women seemed attracted to the boats and fishermen. There was a very nice youngster in Galway who liked to come on board and chat with us in the galley. She was a student in University College, Galway (UCG), studying marine biology, full of fun and laughter. We became concerned for her, as some of the men about the boats might take advantage. Our crew watched out for her. Fishermen are generally a decent lot. We only had to warn off one character who was becoming a nuisance.

Occasionally, women who came to watch us land our catch would ask if they could come out for a trip. If our skipper had no objections, and the weather was fine, two or three would sail with us on a short trip. Bunks on fishing trawlers are somewhat confined. But they might be shared, if a woman so desired. On one such trip the belt broke on the generator, which meant we had no electric power for our fish finder, radar or navigator. We had no spare belt. The skipper radioed the other boats, but to no avail. As we were contemplating having to go ashore early, I had an idea. I got a pair of tights from one of our guests. We pleated the tights into a rope of sorts, stopped the engine, and fitted it in place of the generator belt. We made the loop very small, allowing that it would stretch when we adjusted for strain. It worked. And we were able to continue our trip. We got a second pair of tights and made another rope, just in case. But the first one held, and we finished our trip, very glad that our guests were aboard. The story got about the fishing fleet. And some months later when another trawler had a broken belt they called us on the radio looking to borrow a pair of tights, much to the disgust of our skipper who said we were the laughing stock of the fleet.

Some skippers/owners were very decent, but others behaved like dictators on their trawlers. They treated their deckhands with open contempt and often paid them below what was due. A movement started to unionise deckhands, and I became active in that cause. Deckhands from different fishing ports got together and we approached the Irish Transport and General Workers' Union for representation. The union set up a Fishermen's Branch. The more reactionary skippers/owners began muttering about 'communists' being on the pier. I was considered to be one such agitator. But we carried on, regardless. During one agitation, by the whole fishing industry, the ports were blockaded. The Killybegs deckhands elected me to be their representative.

A meeting with government officials about the fishing industry was being held at a hotel in Killybegs. But we deckhands were not informed, only hearing about it just before it was about to begin. I went to the hotel, and in to the meeting. My own skipper made room for me and I sat down. Then another skipper stood and demanded that I be ejected from the meeting, and several other skippers loudly agreed. My skipper stood and defended me, stating that they would have to forcibly eject him too, as he would defend my right to be present. This brought several more skippers to their feet in my defence. The reactionaries sat down again, muttering to themselves, and the meeting got under way. Not all of those who defended me agreed with me, but they defended my right to be present as a representative of the deckhands. It was an exciting afternoon.

I also attended a conference on the fishing industry in Glenties, a town not far from Killybegs. At lunch I was seated at a table across from Niall Blaney, TD. Conversation was light and easy, and interesting, but I observed that he would look at me keenly from time to time. Eventually he asked if he had met me before. I reminded him about getting the lift from him in the state car in 1959. He laughed, and seemed to remember it well. I think he was the only parliamentarian who attended the conference that day. The remainder seemed to have very little interest in the fishing world. Nothing much came of these meetings, but at least the deckhands were unionised.

Differences arose within the leadership of the Official republican movement. A move was made against Séamus Costello, another ex-internee, and he was ejected from the IRA. Although inactive, I was still an IRA member. Upon being called to an IRA meeting, I was instructed to vote to oust Costello from Sinn Féin, as the leadership wanted him removed from Sinn Féin as well. There and then I resigned from the IRA. Some weeks later I attended the Official Sinn Féin Convention in Dublin, where Costello's ejection was being orchestrated. During the convention I publicly resigned from Sinn Féin as well, disgusted with what was happening. A number of people left the Officials with Séamus Costello and formed The Irish Republican Socialist Party (IRSP) with Costello as its leader. The Irish National Liberation Army (INLA), an armed organisation, was also set up. I had no part in the setting up of the new groups, and did not join with them either. I knew Séamus Costello well, having worked with him in the movement. He was a strong-willed, charismatic figure and quickly gathered a following around him. But my earlier experience taught me to be wary of the 'follow the leader' syndrome and I deliberately stayed away from the new development.

Early in 1975 I was approached by some old comrades, then members of the IRSP, and asked to join. After years of political activity it can be hard to stay away. I agreed to join, and was quickly elected to the National Executive. Bernadette McAlliskey was also on the Executive. In the summer of 1975 she was scheduled to go to Europe on a speaking tour, on behalf of the party, but was unable to go due to pregnancy. The Executive was in a quandary, as a speaking tour represented a great opportunity for the party.

At the time, the *Septemar* was tied up for repairs and painting. I was drawing unemployment benefit and this was my only income while the boat was tied up. When no one else on the Executive could do the tour, I agreed to go, but only on condition that Clarrie would receive payment of the equivalent of my unemployment benefit each week from the party. I couldn't go away and leave her without any income to look after our four children – Anna was 10, Thomas was 7, Lulu was 6 and John was 4. Costello and the Executive agreed. Clarrie was not at all pleased when I told her that I would be away for six weeks, but I tried to re-assure her that everything would be alright and that she would receive money each week.

I was part of a group of three speakers: one for the Provos, one for People's Democracy, and myself for the IRSP. We each spoke, showing the different perspectives on the Irish struggle. The tour covered twenty-four venues over six weeks through Holland, Belgium, Germany, Austria and Switzerland. We met up in Amsterdam and travelled from there by minibus. It was very intense, and sometimes before I'd speak I'd have to check which city I was in, so as not to say the wrong place. We were very well received and mostly spoke to a young audience, varying in number from place to place.

While on the tour Clarrie contacted me to tell me that she had received no money from Costello or the party. This was very upsetting for me, as well as for her. I contacted Costello and told him that if she did not immediately receive the payments as agreed, as guaranteed by him and the party, I would return to Ireland, abandoning the remainder of the tour. I was assured that it was an oversight, which would be rectified that day. Meanwhile, continuing the tour I met a lot of people who expressed interest in the Irish situation. I gave a number of people my contact information, as well as the address of the IRSP in Dublin. Before I had even arrived home, a few young German women called to our home in Killybegs, asking for me. This contributed further to the strain between me and Clarrie, who was convinced that I had been sleeping with women everywhere on the tour. Actually, during the six-week tour I slept with women on two occasions, but I made no mention of those indiscretions. To make matters worse, the party commitment to provide funds for my family when I was away was only partially fulfilled, leaving Clarrie and the children short of the necessities.

I understood how Clarrie distrusted me, and her upset with me having been away and her being let down by the IRSP, all of which was complicated by the German visitors whom I barely knew. But I could not see that it was my entire fault. Our relationship became cold and our home life became more difficult. I returned to fishing and at least had that to occupy me, but Clarrie was at home and without any relief. When I came ashore and went up home I felt uneasy and sought refuge in the pub and alcohol. It was a very difficult time for everybody. To further complicate my life a crisis was approaching in the IRSP and I had a lot of meetings to attend.

In November 1975, about half of the National Executive publicly resigned from the IRSP. I was one of those resigning. I was not prepared to continue in an organisation where control was vested in a leader rather than in an elected Executive, and where armed struggle was not subject to political direction from an Executive. At the time my sympathies were with those engaged in the armed struggle, but I could not bring myself to join the Provos. I could not be part of a bombing campaign where prior warnings were given, which depended upon the RUC, as part of the British authorities, to act properly. I had learned from my previous experience not to rely on someone else to do what I expected of them. That was the end of my participation in any political group or organisation. Nevertheless, the police still kept a watch on me. Whenever anything happened in the west that might have a subversive connection they would check me out. And if I was ashore they might arrest me and detain me for up to forty-eight hours, as usual.

I changed boats and went fishing with Jackie Meehan on his 75-footer the *Sheanne*, a Norwegian-built trawler, and a fine sea boat. Fishing herring with Jackie could be very exciting. We were mid-water trawling, in pairs. Two trawlers would tow a large trawl net between and behind the boats. If fish became scarce out off the shore we often needed to work very close in, going into small coves and bays to catch a shoal of herring. This might take us very close to the rocks, under towering sea cliffs. I loved the work, the danger, the excitement, and the thrill of taking a bag of herring, where other boats might not dare venture.

On one occasion we landed our catch early and sailed again, before the rest of the fleet. Jackie decided to check the waters at Carrigan Head near Sliabh League, an area known to us as 'the north side'. We marked a huge shoal of herring sitting tight on a big peak of rock on the bottom. Any attempt to try for them would mean that we would wreck our net on that high rocky peak. The two boats slipped into Teelan and tied up at the pier with our lights off. Teelan is just around the corner, so to speak, from Carrigan Head. It is a small harbour, not usually frequented by trawlers. The two skippers consulted together and decided to lie there until the tide turned, when the fish would likely swim away from that peak. It was vital that we keep radio silence, and not show any lights, in case some of the other trawlers might spot us. They had, by then, sailed out from Killybegs. And we could hear some of them speculating as to where we had headed to fish. The 'north side' had been slack for several days, and the fleet headed away west towards the Stags Rocks, off the north Mayo coast.

As it came near to high tide we slipped out of Teelan and went in search of the shoal of herring. And sure enough they were away from that peak. We shot away our net, and after a short tow hauled up a big bag of herring, which filled our boat. Our partner then shot his net with similar results. We maintained radio silence and communicated between the two boats by walkie-talkie only. We were ashore and had our catches landed for first market the following morning – and got good prices for them.

Our two crews were sworn to secrecy about where we caught the fish. As other boats came into port we told them we had been fishing out west. While the other boats were still landing their catches, which were much less than we'd had, we sailed again. Maintaining radio silence, we went north again to check out that peak off Carrigan Head. We repeated our manoeuvre of the previous evening, slipping into Teelan to wait for high tide and hoping the rest of the fleet would not locate what we had come to regard as 'our fish'. As the fleet had not seen us out west, they sailed north, without spotting 'our fish' or us, and when high tide came they were well beyond Glen Head. Out of sight, we filled our two boats yet again. We steamed for Killybegs, showing no lights until were well clear of 'our spot', and were the first boats to land again that morning, getting good prices for our catch. On the next sailing, as we were hauling our catch we were seen by another pair of trawlers and that was the end of 'our spot'. But we did very well out of it, and such manoeuvres added to the excitement of our work.

With all the children now in school, Clarrie secured employment with a semi-government organisation as a project worker in County Donegal. She earned well, the work was interesting, and she was very good at it. It also took her out of the house and gave her an outside interest. I tried to help her by being home as much as I could, preparing dinner, etc. The children were wonderful, and the older ones looked out for the younger. I loved being there when they came home from school, but fishing is not conducive to being home on a regular basis. And my growing addiction to alcohol was no help either.

Fishing was hard work, and often dangerous. But I loved it. The hours were long, with sleep scarce; we were often close to exhaustion. But there were magical moments too. One cold frosty winter morning we were hauling our net out off the north Mayo coast. There was a big swell at the time. We did not have power blocks or the machinery common to trawlers today. We were lined along the rail, hauling the net by hand. As the boat dipped down into the trough we would haul like demons, and when she rose up on the crest we would hold tight to the net, using the rail for purchase. Then as she dipped again we would haul rapidly. The crew worked together. Our collective strength, experience and co-operation made for harmony among us. That particular morning we were facing east, and the gannets were diving to try to grab herring from the net mesh. Gannets are beautiful, graceful sea birds. They hover high above, searching for prey. And when they dive, with a loud 'caw', they fold back their large wings, hitting the water at great speed, like a javelin. They go down, and turn back to the surface to catch their prey. As we dipped into a trough in the swell, we saw clearly a gannet dive into the next swell, go deep, turn upward, take a herring from the net and return to the surface again. With the morning light shining through the water it was crystal clear, and very beautiful. We all paused in wonder, and my heart filled with the gift of that magical moment.

One night in November 1976 I was on watch with Jackie in the wheelhouse of the *Sheanne*. Fishing was slack, and we were dodging about in search of a spot of herring. We were in the sound of Rathlin O'Birne Island, near Malin Beg, when the radio crackled to life.

'Mayday! Mayday! This is Ted Carbery on the *Carraig Úna*. We are on the rocks at Rathlin O'Birne Island. Mayday! Mayday!'

Jackie immediately got on the radio, calling Ted. But there was no further communication. He then called Gerry, our partner on the *Rising Tide*, who had also heard the Mayday call. He was at the north end of the island. And as neither of us had seen the *Carraig Úna*, Gerry steamed to the west side of the island from the north, while we steamed south around the island to the west side. I alerted our crew to the situation and returned to the wheelhouse. Jackie had alerted the rescue service and the rest of the fleet.

As we rounded the south side of the island our spotlight picked out an unopened life raft in its casing floating past. We searched to the north along the west side of the island, our spotlight scanning the rocks. Then we spotted the mast of the *Carraig Úna* sticking out of the water; the rest of the boat was under water. Jackie, skilfully and carefully, brought the *Sheanne* as close as he could to the stricken vessel. There was a swell up that night. Our crew lined the rail, with lines, life rings and boat hooks ready, as we scanned the heaving sea. Suddenly a big swell lifted the *Carraig Úna* half out of the water. And as the sea dropped, she smashed back down on to the ledge where she had hit. She broke in two, and disappeared. We were horrified that we had not seen any of her crew, who all went down in her.

Gerry was also there with the *Rising Tide*. The rest of the fleet were soon on the scene, all searching the area in the vain hope of finding someone. We picked up one of the *Carraig Úna*'s life rings and eventually headed back to Killybegs heartbroken over the tragedy. We knew them all, every one of them.

The following morning I was assigned as one of a search party along the shore. We reported to the Garda inspector directing operations from the Glenbay Hotel. We set out around the Ross More, a headland looking out on Rathlin O'Birne Island. As we searched, I spotted two figures coming back towards us, Tom Hegarty and Mick McGinley, two local men totally versed with nature and the sea on that shore. I knew them well from when I had lived nearby and I had great respect for their judgement. When they told me that we would find nothing at that time of day I believed them. They had gone out at 6 a.m. and searched the shore, as that was when they reckoned it would have been possible to find something. They suggested that if we went to a cove near Glen Head then something might just float in there in an hour or two.

I went back to the hotel and informed the inspector, who gathered a few men. With a Garda in charge we drove to the north side of Glencolmcille and, leaving our cars, we climbed to the cove. Shortly after we arrived, some fish boxes and planking floated into the cove, but sadly that was all we saw. All five fishermen were lost, and their bodies were not recovered. The whole community was devastated, and mourned their loss for a long time. There was an announcement on radio and television that there would be an official investigation into the tragedy. There may have been such an investigation, but if there was, the skipper and crew who were first on the scene, and who had witnessed the *Carraig Úna* break in two, were not interviewed.

There was much speculation about how an experienced skipper could put his boat on the rocks at that place, practically under the lighthouse on the island. The *Evelyn Marie* and her crew had been lost at the same place the year before. How could such accidents happen, we wondered. We could only conclude that, for some unknown reason, the boats' instruments, navigator and radar were giving wrong readings, and/or the lighthouse was showing a clear light erroneously. It remained a mystery. A few years later I heard a rumour that an experimental atomic-powered light had been fitted in that lighthouse, and that it was taken out and replaced shortly after the loss of the *Carraig Úna*. It was reckoned that such a light could play havoc with trawlers' electronic equipment.

9

When the boat was not out fishing and tied at the pier, we'd sometimes disappear 'for a pint' out of town. That in itself was not a problem. And we would only be away for a few hours. But it could become a binge and last for days. On one such binge, myself and my shipmate Art found ourselves in Galway drinking and neither of us had any memory of getting there. This was some five days later. We thought the boat must be at Galway docks and were surprised that we could not find it there. As luck would have it, a fisherman from Aran who was working on a boat in Killybegs happened along. He told us the *Sheanne* was actually in Killybegs, and we got a lift home with him. We made a laugh of it all. And I thought it was not unusual, that such things simply happened. I know now, however, that it was not at all normal. And on reflection, there was nothing funny about it.

When we had landed and put out our catch, it seemed the most natural thing to go to the pub for a pint or two. The repartee and camaraderie in the pub was somehow soothing and very enjoyable. It felt good to relax with friends over a few pints. It did not take much inducement to have another drink, just one more for the road. Sometimes that would do, and I'd go up home to my family for a few hours before we'd sail again. Unfortunately, though, that was not always the case, and I'd often find myself still drinking when it was time to go back to the boat. As booze got a grip on me it became much harder to leave the pub, or pass one by. It astonishes me today, as I look back, to realise that I did not seem to be aware of what was happening to me. I loved my wife, I loved my children, and loved being with them. Yet I could not forego a drink if opportunity arose.

Sometimes I could have one or two and go home. But, with increasing frequency, one or two drinks would set me off on a binge, which could last for days. I could go down the town to buy the newspaper, with no thought of drinking, and find myself in a pub with a whiskey in front of me. Or I could go into a pub to have one pint for the thirst, and end up on a binge lasting days, without knowing the how or the why of it, and not even seeing anything unusual about such behaviour. I did not understand it and I would become filled with shame and guilt, and huge anger at myself. I began to have blackouts; often I would not even remember going for a drink. I would come out of a blackout in a different premises, or even a different town, not knowing how I came to be there. I was becoming a chronic alcoholic and did not know it.

There seems to be an invisible line between social and alcoholic drinking, and somewhere in my drinking I crossed that line. I went from enjoying a casual few drinks with friends to being addicted to it. And even in my addiction I did not know I was addicted. That is the nature of alcoholism; the last person to realise they have the disease is the very person who has it. Strength, will power, intelligence, status or position are of no significance once a person is gripped by the disease of alcoholism. That is the reality. I progressed from being a casual social drinker to being a compulsive addict.

I sometimes think the progression can be traced by how I was the morning after. At first a glass of water would suffice, if my mouth or throat felt dry. Then I went from needing a glass of beer to a pint of beer, to a small whiskey, to a large whiskey. I went from having a clear head to having hangovers, the shakes, retching and shivering, desperately seeking 'the cure', 'the hair of the dog', the illusion and delusion that another drink or two would put things right. On one occasion, in the 'horrors', I went for the cure to a pub where I was not known. There were a dozen or so other people in the pub when I entered. Ignoring them, I went to the bar and waited impatiently for the barman to serve me. I ordered a whiskey and some water, as I could not be sure the whiskey would stay down if I drank it straight. The barman put my drink on the bar in front of me and a small jug of water beside it. I gripped the glass, resting my forearm on the bar to stop my hand shaking. Each time I tried to pour water from the jug into the glass my shakes were such that they tinkled together and I had to put them down again. After several attempts the barman came over. 'Let me do that for you, sir.'

'Fuck off and leave me alone,' I snapped.

He backed away, and after several more attempts I managed to tip a little water into the whiskey. Taking a deep breath I raised it to my lips and took a sip. And the whole bar burst into applause. Unknown to me, everyone had been watching my performance with bated breath. I drank my drink, and as it settled I left that bar to go somewhere else, again where I would not be known.

One summer the boat went fishing off the Scottish coast. We worked out of Greencastle in north Donegal, and as we headed home to Killybegs we diverted to Buncrana, where Fleadh Ceol na hÉireann (National Traditional Music Festival) was on that weekend. I became separated from the crew, met some drinking friends and a binge started. We found a pub with a sort of nook, a corner behind the door at the end of the bar. There were about seven or eight of us, drinking and chatting and laughing. There was good music playing. Sometimes someone would sing. We were all enjoying ourselves. The crew found me on Wednesday. They tricked me into getting into their car pretending there was a good session in a pub out the road. Then they drove me back to the boat and we went out fishing.

At the time I could not see the hurt and worry my behaviour inflicted upon my family. I would arrive home, as if I had not been missing from them for days, unable to even begin to explain myself or what had happened. I became a very lonely, isolated person, unable to properly communicate, even with myself. I knew something was wrong. But I could not see that it was me – and booze. It never entered my head that booze was my problem. Clarrie became ill and had to go into hospital. Her mother came to look after the children. I was totally inadequate to the situation. My existence was dominated by booze.

Gerry, a friend who had fished and drunk with me, got sober and bought a trawler. It can be difficult getting a good crew when starting off with a new boat, so I left the *Sheanne* and went fishing with Gerry. He was a very good skipper and we worked well together. He tried to talk to me about my drinking, coaxing me to go with him to a meeting. He might as well have been talking to the wall at that time, because I could not hear what he was saying. Being sick from booze is one thing, but waking up in my bunk with the boat heaving and rolling in a rough sea, to the stench of diesel and lubrication oil and stale water in the bilges, was absolutely the pits. Having to go up on deck to shoot away the net with my head lifting, my stomach churning and my nerves raw was an awful experience. At such times I would swear, 'Never again'. But as soon as we headed back to port, the anticipation of a drink would catch hold of me and my previous state would fade from my mind completely. It was weird, and totally incomprehensible to me at the time. After fishing with Gerry for some months he announced he would have to fish at weekends. And I left that boat.

Home life had become a living hell. One day, Clarrie asked me to sit down as she wanted to talk to me. She spoke at length about my behaviour and its effect on family life. She asked me if I could change. I could not even fully understand the import of what she was saying. Eventually she said it was over. She wanted me out of their lives and told me to leave, not just our home but Killybegs as well. She said it would be better that way, for her and for our children.

My mind was addled from booze and I accepted Clarrie's position. My first feeling was a curious sense of relief, which I did not understand. This was followed by deep feelings of shame, regret and loss. I was moving in a sort of daze, unable to see clearly what had happened and what was happening. I could not even comprehend that if I left Killybegs, as Clarrie wanted me to do, I would not be able to see the children. A trawler from Kilronan, on the Aran Islands off Galway, was in Killybegs at the time being refitted. I got a berth on it, with my one bag of belongings, and we sailed for Kilronan, where we would be based. Tony Mór, the skipper, was a decent man and a fair one. Without my having to go into the nitty-gritty of my situation, he made me comfortable on his boat.

I existed in a sort of emotional limbo during this period, lost to my family and my family lost to me. I was going through the motions of doing my job on the boat, drinking when I could and not even enjoying the booze. It was a weird time for me – and a very lonely time too. I was only allowed to see the children on alternate Saturdays, from 10 a.m. to 6 p.m. And those days, when I could get to see them, were heartbreaking. I had to be in Killybegs to collect them at 10 a.m. and return them at 6 p.m. The tension was almost unbearable. Then I'd have to return to Galway that evening. On a fine day we could do something outdoors. But on a wet day, and with little money, there was nowhere to take them. And that was the most difficult part. I deeply regret that I was not good at communicating with my children; and I know it was very difficult for them too.

What with fishing out of Kilronan and trying to get to see the children, I was not drinking as much. Then one weekend in Galway I met some friends, went on a binge, and missed the boat. The binge lasted ten days or more. We drank almost around the clock, only getting a few hours' sleep at odd times and eating nothing. One night in a pub a smiling woman approached me and we talked a while. Afterwards all I could remember about her was her smiling, brown eyes. I was not sure if it had happened or if I'd imagined her. The following night she appeared again. We talked some more and arranged to meet the next day in the Cellar Bar at 4 p.m.

I spent that night on a boat. I slept fitfully, with terrible dreams, and woke several times cold, sweating and shivering. I woke once at 9.25 a.m., and slept again. And a complete day passed in my dream. When I woke again and looked at my watch, it was 9.26 a.m. One minute of actual time had passed, while I dreamed a whole day. I could not grasp the significance of it all, and thought I must surely be crazy. My brain was addled and I was in the horrors, nerves screaming and unable to stop shivering. I lay there for a long time, and then got up and dressed. I somehow got myself up on the pier safely and headed up the town for 'the cure'. I met a friend and we went to Garavan's, sipped on a brandy and port until my system settled a bit and I was able to focus on the day, which I discovered was a Friday. I went to the college to have a shower, as there was no shower on board, changed my clothes and returned to the boat. I rested awhile and then went up town to the Cellar Bar to see if what I remembered was real or a delusion.

I was sitting there alone, on a seat away from the bar with a cup of black coffee when she arrived, confirming that she was not a figment of my imagination or hallucination. Eva was her name, and we went to the Corrib Great Southern Hotel where we had a sauna. I knew from experience that the sauna would help my recovery, as the alcohol seeped out through my pores. While in the sauna a man entered and remarked that it smelled like a pub. Eva told me later that she was fearful I might have a heart attack when I was in the cold shower after the sauna. She insisted I have a 'pint shandy' (beer and lemonade) then, to restore some liquid to my body. She drove us to Clare, and the Burren, and we spent the night in a hotel in Gort. I slept deeply, for the first time in weeks. She drove me to Rossaveal where I caught a boat to Kilronan to rejoin the trawler and return to fishing. Eva's interest in me seemed quite remarkable, and I was heartened by it. When I came ashore the following Friday she was on the pier to meet me. We spent the weekend together, wandering about the city and walking along the shore. It was a nice change for me. We met regularly and got on well together. Her companionship helped fill the void left by my estrangement from my family.

Some weeks later she and I rented a house outside Galway and moved in together. I left the trawler and got a berth skippering an old car ferry called *Severn Princess*, ferrying cargo to the three Aran Islands. The *Princess* was owned by a small company called Oceanic Services, which had the contract to carry goods to the islands. She had a crew of three, two deckhands, Paddy and Seán, and myself as skipper. They were responsible for loading and storing cargo aboard, while my job was to take the boat safely to our destination and supervise the discharge of our cargo. Then I'd take the boat back to Rossaveal and berth her there. Rossaveal was about thirty minutes' drive from home.

Usually we sailed every second day to one or other of the islands. Inis Oírr and Inis Meáin piers were tidal and our schedule to these islands was dictated by the tides. We would arrive about two hours before high tide, discharge our cargo and be ready to sail again no later than two hours after high tide. Such landings could be tricky. If there was a swell, I often needed to use our engines as well as shore ropes to keep the boat steady while we discharged our cargo. Kilronan on Inis Mór was not tidal, and much easier for our purposes.

On Wednesday 2 July 1980 I delivered a cargo of 4,000 concrete blocks to Kilmurvey Pier, on Inis Mór, for a fisherman who was about to build a house close to Kilmurvey. This saved him the difficulty of transporting his concrete blocks from Kilronan to Kilmurvey by tractor and trailer. But Kilmurvey was a small inlet, and the pier was tidal so we did not sail from Rossaveal until 4.30 p.m. I manoeuvred the boat safely to the pier, through what were unknown waters for me, and we successfully unloaded our cargo. This was the first time in about fifty years that a boat of our size had landed at Kilmurvey, and there was quite a gathering of islanders for the event. As the sea was calm I had a pint in the nearby pub with the owner of the concrete blocks, who gave me a tip for Paddy and Seán. They were well pleased as we sailed away from Kilmurvey around midnight for Rossaveal, the islanders waving farewell.

Oceanic Services had a car at our disposal, and Seán drove us back from Rossaveal, dropping me home about two o'clock the following morning.

10

During this period I thought I was controlling my drinking, mostly going out with Eva for a social drink with friends. We agreed that whoever was driving could not drink. Eva did most of the driving on such occasions. I went to a dentist to have my teeth seen to, something I should have attended to years earlier. I visited the dentist a number of times and he built two new teeth onto roots that were sound. This was a great piece of work. He told me they were fine for eating and normal activity, but not to get any blows on them for about two months to allow them really harden.

My life had settled in to a more consistent and manageable pattern. Maybe it was because Eva was part of my drinking, and helped facilitate our lifestyle in that regard. But I missed my children, and could not get to see them as often as I wished. Sometimes the days allocated to me to visit them did not coincide with me having the funds necessary to make the long trip. I was deeply upset about having so little access to them and the existing arrangements in that regard.

I decided to go to Killybegs and try talking with Clarrie about it all. I told my boss that I would be off work on Monday, figuring to see Clarrie while the children were still in school. Eva left for work that morning and I headed off on my own for Killybegs. I made the mistake of stopping in a local pub to buy a bottle of whiskey, 'for the road'. That was Monday 7 July 1980. My journey to Killybegs, and my best intentions regarding my children, became yet another binge of drinking in and around Galway, which lasted almost twelve days. Those days and nights passed in a drunken haze, eating nothing and sleeping fitfully, sometimes in deep melancholy, sometimes trying to feel happy at the world, and all the time depressed by my situation.

Somewhere during those twelve days I lost my car. I vaguely remember lending it to someone, but I cannot be sure about that. I met Peadar, a drinking buddy, who had a house near the Galway racecourse, and I stayed there. Sometimes we'd just drink in the house. He liked to smoke a bit of dope, but I preferred booze, which seemed fair enough at the time. I would drink until I'd pass out, wake up again and continue where I'd left off. What astonishes me now is that I did not see anything strange or unusual in my behaviour, even as the enjoyment had gone from drinking. It was like I had no choice, and simply had to keep drinking until I could drink no more. Peadar told me he heard in a pub that the Gardaí might be looking for me, about some robbery and shooting which happened on Monday 7 July. At first I thought he was joking, but gradually it sank in through my addled brain that he was serious. A bank had been robbed in Ballaghaderreen in County Roscommon on the date in question and two Gardaí had been killed. Quite often, when incidents happened in the west of Ireland the Gardaí would, as they say, 'round up the usual suspects'. And if there was any political or subversive element in it they would often arrest and detain me for up to forty-eight hours.

As I began to come out of the binge and think a bit rationally again I realised that I had begun the binge on the same day as the crimes had been committed. I knew they had nothing to do with me and I was not unduly worried. I decided that I would go to see my then solicitor, Leonard Silke. Together he and I would go to the Gardaí to sort things out. It would be obvious to them I had nothing to do with the crimes. But Peadar said I could never get across town to Leonard's office without being spotted. He suggested I shave my beard and cut and dye my hair so I would not be recognised before seeing my solicitor. Although this was completely alcoholic thinking, it seemed reasonable to me at the time. Peadar got some dye and cut my hair, and helped me shave my beard off. I was still in the shakes from drinking and needed to recuperate a bit before venturing out onto the streets. Peadar reckoned he would contact Eva, and also my solicitor, and let them know I was alright and I would see them in a few days. This would give me a chance to recover a little from the DTs.

But it did not happen that way. A couple of days later, on Saturday 19 July, I was arrested in Peadar's house at 3 p.m. Detectives entered the house through a rear window. I was lying on a bed upstairs, half asleep, trying to overcome the effects of my binge when a man entered the bedroom and asked me who I was. I told him my name. He called to detectives downstairs and then told me he was arresting me under Section 30 of the Offences Against the state Act, 1939, for the murder of a Garda. I was allowed to put on boots and a sweater, before being hustled down the stairs, out of the house and into the back of an unmarked police car with a detective on each side of me. I was somewhat in shock and trying not to shiver, being still in the shakes after my drinking.

My whole body screamed silently for a drink, even though I did not know if I could hold down a drink at all. It was a weird situation, squeezed in between two detectives in the back of a car, trying to hold myself together and not to let them see how shattered I was. Nerves screaming, head splitting, body shaking, stomach burning, eyes red and watering, mouth and throat so dry and parched, I was a wreck. The detectives would not stop interrogating me as we drove to the Garda station. I tightened up within myself and said nothing. I was determined to hold on for dear life, and not show any weakness.

When we arrived at Eglinton Street Garda station I was taken to a room and immediately ordered to take off my clothes. This was most unusual behaviour. I stood naked as detectives moved around me inspecting my body, as if they were looking for something in particular, which baffled me. I learned later that the man they were looking for had been wounded. They seemed puzzled, and disappointed, and told me to dress again.

At 4 p.m. two detectives came in and introduced themselves. I recognized their names; they were part of what was commonly termed at the time 'the heavy gang' based in Dublin. They started interrogating me about the robbery in Ballaghaderreen, County Roscommon on Monday 7 July 1980 and the killing of two Gardaí. I gave them my name and address and date of birth. Then I asked to see my solicitor, and would not answer any further questions. This was how I always responded to being arrested.

The detectives told me that three men had robbed a bank in Ballaghaderreen and got away from the town. But as they fled through the countryside their car collided with a marked Garda car and in the subsequent shooting two Gardaí were killed. They told me that this was capital murder and that I could be hanged for the killings. I told them that I was innocent, and knew nothing of these matters.

From then on I was interrogated continually by teams of detectives, some of whom slapped, punched and kicked me. I was generally treated very aggressively. I had a visit from my solicitor, who told me to answer no questions, which was my policy anyway. Detectives took my fingerprints and samples of my hair. They took away my clothing and gave me jeans, a sweater and canvas shoes to wear. They also swabbed my hands for firearms residue and photographed me. This was not the routine 'question and release' I was used to going through.

The interrogations continued for over twelve hours, from 4 p.m. on Saturday until 4.30 a.m. on Sunday morning. I was put into a dirty cell that smelled of vomit, sweat and shit. The blanket on the bunk was putrid. They kept rattling the door, or banging on it, so I could not sleep. Huddled on the bunk shivering, I detoxed from the alcohol. My body ached. It was difficult to get into a comfortable

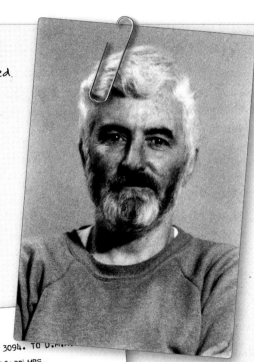

Myself, photographed whilst in prison.

Circular issued to all Gardaí the day before my arrest.

8769+
ER
24543+
4543 GSDA EI
OMMUNICATIONS CENTRE. D/CASTLE. MESSAGE NO 3094. TO D.....

CIR. PER CODE 41/14.   DAZE 18/7/80.   18.30 HRS.
===

ESSAGE FROM ASSISTANT COMMISSIONER JOHN PAUL MC MAHON, CRIME
INVESTIGATION BRANCH. GARDA HEADQUARTERS.

RE   MURDER OF TWO GARDAI OUTSIDE BALLAGHADREEN, CO ROSCOMMON ON 7.7.8
7.TH JULY 1980.
===

TO EACH DIVISIONAL OFFICER

THE UNDER MENTIONED MAN IS WANTED FOR INTERVIEW IN CONNECTION WITH
THE MURDER OF THE TWO GARDAI ON 7.7.80.

PETER PRINGLE, 41 YRS, DOB 10.11.38 AT DUBLIN. 6'2'' GOOD BUILD
SHOULDER LENGTH BROWN HAIR GOING GREY AND WEARING A BROWN/GREY
BEARD.   THE POSSIBILITY OF THE HAIR STYLE BEING ALTERED SHOULD
NOT BE OVERLOOKED.

PRINGLE IS A FISHERMAN BY OCCUPATION. HE IS ADDICTED TO DRINK AND
DRUGS.

PLEASE SEE PHOTOGRAPHS PUBLISHED IN FOGRA TORA SUPPLEMENT OF 12.7.80
AND NATIONAL CRIMINAL INTELLIGENCE OFFICE BULLETIN DATED 15.7.80

N.B   AN INTENSIVE AND COMPREHENSIVE SEARCH FOR THIS MAN SHOULD BE
UNDERTAKEN IN ALL DIVISIONS, COMMENCING EARLY ON MONDAY MORNING
THE 21/7/80.

PARTICULAR ATTENTION SHOULD BE PAID TO BOATS, SEAPORTS, AND OTHER F
FISHING AREAS. ALSO CARAVANS, CAMPING SITES, HOTELS, GUEST HOUSES,
AND THE PREMISES OF KNOWN OR SUSPECTED ASSOCIATES.

IT IS NOT CONSIDERED NECCESSARY TO EMPHASISE THE SERIOUSNESS OF THE
CASE UNDER INVESTIGATION AND IT IS EXPECTED THAT EACH AND EVERY MEMB
OF THE FORCE WILL USE HIS BEST ENDEVOURS IN THE PURSUIT OF PRINGLE.
IT SHOULD BE NOTED THAT HE IS CONSIDERED DANGEROUS AND MAY BE ARMED.

HE SHOULD BE APPROACHED WITH CAUTION, SEARCHED IMMEDIATLY AND
DETAINED UNDER SECTION 30 OFFENCES AGAINST THE STATE ACT 1939.

ANY INTELLEGENCE FORTHCOMING SHOULD BE COMMUNICATED TO DETECTIVE
SUPERINTENDENT JOHN COURTNEY, INCIDENT ROOM CASTLEREA, GDA STATION
TELEPHONE (094) 71466 OR 71420.
MESSAGE ENDS. DATED AT 6PM ON FRIDAY THE 18TH JULU 1980.
SIGNED

     JOHN PAUL MC MANON ASST/COMMISSIONER CRIME.

SENDER PAT C DAVY D/SGT DCRO.
5740 GSTB EI

COMMUNICATIONS PSE RE TRANS PER COD 41.14

Certificate of the DDP sending me to the Special Criminal Court.

OFFENCES AGAINST THE STATE ACT, 1939.

Person intended to be charged: Peter Pringle

Certificate of the Director of Public Prosecutions under Section 47 (2) of the above-named Act, with direction under Section 47 (1) of the said Act.

I, Eamonn M. Barnes, Director of Public Prosecutions, intending to have the above-named person charged with the offences set out in the Schedule hereto which are not scheduled offences under the above-named Act hereby certify that the ordinary Courts are, in my opinion, inadequate to secure the effective administration of justice and the preservation of public peace and order in relation to the trial of the said person on the said charges and direct that the said person in lieu of being charged with the said offences before a Justice of the District Court, be brought before the Special Criminal Court established by the Government on the 30th day of May, 1972 and there charged with the said offences

SCHEDULE

You, Peter Pringle, on the 7th day of July, 1980, at Aghaderry, Loughglynn, County Roscommon, murdered Garda Henry Byrne, he then being a member of the Garda Síochán acting in the course of his duty,
Contrary to Section 1(1) of the Criminal Justice Act, 1964.

You, Peter Pringle, on the 7th day of July, 1980, at the Bank of Ireland, Main Str Ballaghaderreen, County Roscommon, robbed Fintan Donnelly of the sum of £41,000.00 approximately,
Contrary to Section 23 of the Larceny Act, 1916, as inserted by Section 5 of the Criminal Law (Jurisdiction) Act, 1976.

Dated this 21st day of July, 1980.

Signed: Eamonn M. Barnes
DIRECTOR OF PUBLIC PROSECUTIONS.

(875)113487. 5,000. 4-80. F.P.—G20.

P. 25

County of the City of Dublin

Return of Prisoner under Rule Order or Sentence at a Special Criminal Court held in said County commencing on Tuesday day the 13th day of June 19 72

Bill No. 28s/1980

Name Peter Pringle

Date of Conviction 27th November, 1980   Date of Sentence 27th November, 1980

Before whom tried a Special Criminal Court   Where tried Green St., Courthouse, Dublin

Whether pleaded "Guilty" or "Not Guilty": Pleaded "Not Guilty"

CRIME	SENTENCE
COUNT NO. 2. Robbery contrary to Section 23 of the Larceny Act 1916 as inserted by Section 5 of the Criminal Law (Jurisdiction) Act 1976.	To be imprisoned for a period of fifteen years to date from the 27th day of November, 1980

WARRANT

To the Governor of Mountjoy Prison, Dublin

Receive into your custody the body of the above-named person tried and convicted at a Special Criminal/ Court held at Green St., Courthouse in the County of the City of Dublin on the 13th day of June 19 72 and following days. before a Special Criminal Court and cause said person so convicted to undergo the sentence as set out above.

Dated this 27th day of November, 19 80

By Order of the Court.

J. Loughlin
County Registrar for Special Criminal Court

Robbery sentence/ warrant of the Special Criminal Court.

SPECIAL CRIMINAL COURT

AT GREEN STREET COURTHOUSE

DUBLIN

ON THURSDAY THE 27TH DAY OF NOVEMBER, 1980

Before a Special Criminal Court

WHEREAS at a Special Criminal Court holden at the Courthouse Green Street in the County of the City of Dublin on Thursday the 27th day of November in the year of Our Lord one thousand nine hundred and Eighty Peter Pringle was in due course of Law Indicted tried and convicted of having on the 7th day of July 1980 murdered one Henry Byrne he then being a member of An Garda Siochana, acting in the course of his

.D THEREUPON IT WAS ORDERED AND ADJUDGED by the Court as follows:-

COUNT 1 The Sentence and Judgment of the Court are and it is ordered and directed that you Peter Pringle be now, removed from this Court to the Prison in which you were last confined and that you be there detained in custody and that on the 19th day of December one thousand nine hundred and Eighty you there suffer death by execution in the manner rescribed by law and that after such sentence shall have .an carried into effect your body be buried within the precincts of the said Prison.

These are therefore to Command you the Governor of Portlaoise Prison, Portlaoise in the County of Laois in which the said Peter Pringle is now confined that on Friday the 19th day of December in the year of Our Lord one thousand nine hundred and Eighty you take the body of the said Peter Pringle and that you cause execution of the Judgment aforesaid to be done upon the said Peter Pringle in the manner prescribed by law and for you so doing this shall be your sufficient Warrant.

Sealed and dated this 27th day of November in the year of Our Lord one thousand nine hundred and Eighty.

Court transcript.

Court transcript giving my death sentence.

Count 2, the sentence to date from the 27th day of .vember 1980.

PETER PRINGLE COUNT 1 The Sentence and Judgment of the Court are and it is ordered and directed that PETER PRINGLE be now removed from this Court to the Prison in which he was last confined and that he be there detained in custody and that on the 19th day of December 1980 he there suffer death by execution in the manner prescribed by law and that after such sentence shall have been carried into effect his body be buried within the precincts of the said Prison.

PETER PRINGLE to be imprisoned for a period of 15 years on Count 2, the sentence to date from the 27th day of November, 1980.

And on the application of Counsel for the accused Colm O'Shea the Court Doth adjourn the hearing of applications on behalf of each of the accused for Certificates for leave to appeal to Monday the 1st day of December, 1980 at 2 p.m. to enable Counsel to prepare grounds of appeal.

J.J. O'Laughlin
Registrar
Special Criminal Court

The matter again coming on for hearing before the Court on the 1st day of December, 1980 and Counsel for the accused Patrick McCann making application for certificate for leave to appeal (16 grounds stated) Counsel for accused Peter Pringle making application for Certificate for leave to appeal (4 grounds stated) and Counsel for accused Colm O'Shea making application for Certificate for leave to appeal (17 grounds stated) The Court Doth Refuse the application in respect of each accused.

And the Court Doth Refuse the application of Counsel for accused Peter Pringle for liberty for said accused to address the Court.

J.J. O'Laughlin
Registrar
Special Criminal Court.

Notice refusing my application for Leave to Appeal.

Form No. 25.

NOTICE OF RESULT OF APPEAL

COURT OF CRIMINAL APPEAL

The People at the suit of the Director of Public Prosecutions

v

Peter Pringle

To the Department of Justice (Prisons Section).

To the Governor of .... Prison

To the County Registrar for ....

To the Commissioner, Garda Síochána

Take notice that the Court of Criminal Appeal has this day given judgment to the effect following, viz.: Application for leave to appeal against conviction and sentence

Application Refused, the Court in Pursuance of Section 6 (Subsection 2) of the Courts of Justice Act 1928, fixed the 8th. day of June 1981 as the date of execution

Dated 22nd May 1981

Signed W. G. Kenna.

Assistant Registrar.

An Rúnaí
(The Secretary)

(72-76 St. Stephen's Green),

BAILE ÁTHA CLIA.
(Dublin, 2)

Le'n uimhir seo:—
and the following number quoted:-

Telephone (01) 789711

Governor,
Portlaoise Prison.

Re: Patrick McCann
Colm O'Shea
Peter Pringle

I am directed by the Minister for Justice to inform you that the President, on 27 May, 1981, acting on the advice of the Government, commuted to penal servitude for forty years in each case, the sentence of death imposed by the Special Criminal Court on 27 November, 1980 on the above named offenders on their conviction of the murder of Garda Henry Byrne.

I am to add that the decision of the Government to advise the President to commute the sentence was arrived at on the understanding that the full sentence of forty years would be served without remission.

18 June, 1981.

Letter from the Secretary, Department of Justice, to the Governor of Portlaoise Prison, informing him of the commutation of my death sentence to forty years' penal servitude.

A portrait of me painted by the artist
Brian Maguire.

A painting I did whilst in prison.

1-11/92

Dear Freind you do not know
me, or may never have herd
of me. I just want to let
you no that there is some
people woo think of you
  The people that rased this
few bob for you. Where kids
going to schoole in early teens
and midle teens. I do not
know where they herd of you
  I think it was from a shulter
they came and asked me if I new
you. I said I new of you like
the Berugham six the my anvile
seven and so forth. So they
dulsided to do a lyttle bit for
you as they did for them
and it makes me wile so good

to think that there is kids
like this stil around,
  Mabie there stil hope
for this little, Sad Lord
of ours, I dont want to go
on and on So I wile end it here
wishing you all the best, and
hopeing you wile get justes
if there is such a Things.
I hop you understand that
I never went to schoole
The few bob is £65
                    aVid
                    Billy

A letter of support,
which enclosed
a donation, from
Billy.

? **IN THE NAME OF JUSTICE** ?

**The Birmingham Six
The Guildford Four
Judith Ward
Nicky Kelly**

> " First they came for the Jews
> and I did not speak out -
> Because I was not a Jew.
>
> Then they came for the Communists
> and I did not speak out-
> Because I was not a Communist.
>
> Next they came for the Trade Unionists
> and I did not speak out-
> Because I was not a Trade Unionist.
>
> Then they came for me
> and there was no one left -
> To speak out for me."

WHO WILL SPEAK OUT
FOR

PETER PRINGLE

FRAMED IN 1980
FOR CRIMES HE DID NOT COMMIT
NOW **14 YEARS** IN PORTLAOISE PRISON.

PETER PRINGLE SUPPORT GROUP
P.O. Box 3625,
Dublin 3.

Judge sends letter to convicted murderer

By COLM KEENA

A BROTHER of Garda Henry Byrne, killed by a gang of bank robbers in July, 1980, has said that Peter Pringle, convicted of the murder and currently imprisoned in Portlaoise Prison, should be given legal aid to try prove his claim that he is innocent of the crime.

Supreme Court Judge, Seamus Egan, who represented Pringle in his original trial, wrote to the fifty-five-year-old last month and stated that the evidence used to convict him was, in his view, insufficient.

"I also hope the day is not too far off when you will be at liberty," the judge wrote at the end of the short letter, written on Supreme Court notepaper.

Pringle was sentenced to death by the Supreme Court in November, 1980. After an unsuccessful appeal, the sentence against Pringle, and two others, was commuted to forty-years without remission.

Peter Pringle: letter from Supreme Court Judge

Two gardai were shot dead by the raiders of a bank at Ballaghaderreen, Co Roscommon, in July 1980.

The murders happened after the gang's getaway cars rammed a Garda car on a quiet road outside the town.

Garda Henry Byrne was 29-years-old at the time, and the second Garda, Det Garda John Morley, was 38-years-old.

Det Garda Morley was a father-of-three, from Castlerea, and Garda Byrne was a father-of-two, from Knock.

Garda Byrne's wife gave birth to a baby girl three months after the murders.

Although two Gardai were killed in the shoot-out, as usual in such cases the three accused — Pringle, Colm O'Shea, and Patrick McCann — were convicted on just one count of capital murder.

On November 20 last the High Court rejected an attempt by Pringle to have his whole case reopened but the case, said Mr Justice Murphy, had raised matters of such importance he would welcome an appeal to the Supreme Court.

In the event of such an appeal, the judge said he would be anxious the Legal Aid Board would make legal assistance available to Pringle, who has conducted his own case to date.

During his verdict Mr Justice Murphy said: "If the contentions of (Pringle) are correct not only were the criminal proceedings flawed but they were flawed with the result that an innocent man was convicted of the most serious crimes and deprived of his liberty and nearly forfeited his very life."

However Belfast solicitor Ms Padraigin Drinan, who had been giving Pringle legal advice free of charge, says the Legal Aid Board have ignored earlier appeals from the bench that Pringle be given legal assistance.

Pringle hopes to have an appeal heard by the Supreme Court early next year. He has applied again to the Legal Aid Board and is awaiting a decision.

Mr Tom Byrne, of Carraroe, Co Sligo, brother of murdered Garda Byrne, has said his family would not object to Pringle being given legal aid to try prove his claimed innocence.

Mr Justice Seamus Egan

'The evidence used to convict him was insufficient'

"Let him try prove that he has a case. When you think of what happened in England, then you can't be that sure nowadays," said Mr Byrne.

"The evidence seemed to be strong at the time, but if he has a case, then the family would not be against any fair hearing."

Mr Byrne was holidaying with his wife Maureen in England at the time of the killing and did not hear about it until two days later. He got home just in time for the funeral.

"My mother said she had said prayers for the two boys (the gardai) and for the three involved in the killing.

"I'm sure our mother would feel that if he has a case, then why not go ahead with it."

The Byrne family was shocked at first when they read in the newspaper of Pringle trying to overturn his conviction, he said, but when they read of Mr Justice Egan's views,"well he was his barrister in the case, so there must be something."

Mr Byrne said the bitterness was gone now, but that if Pringle was released on some technicality, as against his being proved innocent, that that would be difficult for the family to stomach.

"We would find it very hard if he got out through some loophole in the law."

However, because of the current position with Irish law, Pringle can only reopen his case on points of law as the evidence involved has already been considered by the original court hearing.

This situation will be changed by the Criminal Procedure Bill, currently before the Seanad and due to become law early next year, although the Pringle Supreme Court appeal is still likely to go ahead.

Mr Justice Egan has said he will not preside over the case if and when it reaches the Supreme Court.

Pringle, originally from Ringsend, Dublin, and the son of a garda, had a past involvement in republicanism and was known to the Gardai.

He claims he never said the words which formed the sole basis of his conviction: "I know you know I was involved, but on the advice of my solicitor, I am saying nothing and you will have to prove it all the way."

Pringle says his words in fact were; "I know you think you know I did it..."

In his letter Mr Justice Egan says: "Even taking the alleged words as an admission that you were "involved" this was not, in my opinion, enough to constitute murder and could not be linked with what had been put to you the previous night."

(The statement was allegedly made on the second day of questioning.

During the gunfight with the gardai, Garda Morley fired a number of bullets from an Uzi sub machine gun.

When one of the raiders was arrested, he said his colleague was wounded. This man was the subject of a massive Garda-Army search, as he had been seen running from the scene into nearby woods.

When Pringle was arrested, some days later, he was not wounded. According to Ms Drinan, blood spilled in the garda car did not belong to any of the gardai, or to O'Shea or McCann. It is of a different blood type to Pringle's, she said.

Pringle had been living as a fisherman in Galway at the time of his arrest. His then companion, Ms Eva Anselm, has this week pleaded with Justice Minister Maire Geoghegan-Quinn that Pringle be given temporary release for Christmas. She says he is in good spirits, and confident he will be released.

An article from the Irish Press, Wednesday 22 December 1993.

Peter Pringle freed as case dropped by State

No new trial on murder charge

A COURT freed Peter Pringle in Dublin this afternoon after the State said it was not proceeding with a new trial against him for the murder of a Garda.

During the one minute hearing at the Special Criminal Court, State counsel Mr. George Birmingham B.L. said his instructions were to enter a nolle prosequi.

Counsel for Mr. Pringle, Barry White S.C. said: "I can't object to that."

Mr. Justice Frederick Morris presiding then said the nolle prosequi would be entered and discharged Mr. Pringle.

He left the courthouse shaking hands with his legal team and family members.

He said: "It is a relief. It's nice to see that they have made the right decision for a change. They couldn't have convicted me anyway."

"There are other victims of miscarriages of justice in the system. I would hope that they will take hope from what has happened to me."

Asked about his plans, He said: "I am going back home to Galway to walk on the sea shore and in the mountains."

The Court of Criminal Appeal last week quashed Mr Pringle's original conviction for the murder of Garda Henry Byrne and ordered a new trial.

Mr Pringle was then freed on £60,000 bail by the Special Criminal Court. The court freed him on his own bail of £10,000 and two independent sureties of £25,000 each until today despite Garda objections that he would not stand trial.

Pringle told the court then: "I have absolutely no intention of trying to avoid this trial. It's in my interest, in the interests of my children and in the interests of my loved ones that I defend this case."

Pringle (56), a native of Ringsend, Dublin was convicted at the Special Criminal Court on November 27, 1980 of the capital murder of Garda Henry Byrne following a 23-day trial.

The father of five was sentenced to death but the sentence was later commuted by President Patrick Hillery to 40 years imprisonment without remission.

The trial arose out of a robbery at the Bank of Ireland branch in Ballaghaderreen, Co. Roscommon on July 7, 1980. A three man gang raided the bank and escaped with £41,000 after firing shots.

The raiders' car collided with a Garda patrol car at Shannon's Cross, three miles outside Ballaghaderreen and Garda Byrne (29), who was unarmed, died instantly after the car was blasted with a fusillade of pistol shots and a shotgun blast.

Detective Garda John Morley (38), who was hit with buckshot returned fire with his Uzi submachine gun wounding one of

Peter Pringle . . . no new trial.

the raiders, but he died on the roadside shortly afterwards.

Pringle was the last of three suspects to be arrested. The others were Patrick McCann and Colm O'Shea who are currently serving 40 years sentences for their part in Garda Byrne's murder.

The Court of Criminal Appeal quashed Pringle's conviction last week after ruling that new evidence rendered his conviction unsafe and unsatisfactory.

Peter Pringle told RTE after he was freed on bail that he was savouring his first days of freedom. He said he had missed the countryside, sea and mountains most.

"I have been inside 14 years and 10 months. In that time I have never seen the night sky properly, I have never been on a DART." He hadn't seen dogs or children.

Choking back tears, he said he had never had a private conversation with his children, partner or friends. "That for me is the most painful thing about being in prison."

The best thing about prison was the prisoners he had met in the top-security Portlaoise jail, Mr Pringle said. "They're great people, in particular the small number of people with whom I shared the landing. In my lifetime I have never met more tolerable people."

He said he was "furious" after his conviction and had had to come to terms with death because there was "a good possibility" he would be hanged. Then his sentence was commuted and he had focussed on proving his innocence.

He had studied law and had had to struggle with the authorities to secure a typewriter, legal documents and other materials.

He had begun a civil action in 1992 and that culminated with last week's appeal decision.

Asked how he felt facing into a new trial, Mr Pringle pointed out if his case came under British law there would be no retrial because the British Court of Appeal has ruled a retrial of a case older than three years is not reasonable.

He said: "If they're foolish enough to come again and try to try me again on this, they can't convict me on this."

Emotional Pringle rediscovers privacy

Peter Pringle, after he was released yesterday, with his son.

By Carol Flynn

PETER PRINGLE, whose conviction for the capital murder of a garda was quashed and a retrial ordered, broke down today when he spoke of his first day of freedom in 15 years.

The 56-year-old said his first impressions of Dublin were of big expensive cars, more traffic and larger buildings. But much of his native city remained the same, he observed.

"I noticed a lot of spaces and a lot of apartments. Way back then, it was office blocks they were building but now it's apartments."

Although a Dubliner, he said what he missed most while he faced 40 years of imprisonment without remission in Portlaoise was the countryside. "I missed the ocean because I spent years fishing, I missed the mountains, the smell of the land and the feel of the grass and the sand. I also missed children."

He became emotional when he spoke of how he could never have a private conversation with his children, during visits. "Last night was the first time in 15 years that I had a private word with my son. That for me is the most painful."

He said he survived the system by never allowing the colours and memories of his past life to dim in the grey surroundings of Portlaoise. "I never kept my mind in prison."

Despite losing a huge chunk of his life, he said: "I'm not a bitter man — not now. I used to be, but being bitter is more damaging to me than anyone else."

He spoke of the difficulties he experienced in getting access to books and typewriters while in prison when he attempted to educate himself. He eventually mastered the law sufficiently to defend himself in court.

"One wonders what I would have had in 15 years of freedom. Despair was never far from my shoulder while in prison."

position. After about three hours of dozing fitfully they came for me again. At 8 a.m. they took me from the cell. I just managed to throw cold water on my face at the sink in the hallway before being taken to a room where the interrogation resumed. It went on all morning, except when I got to see my solicitor who insisted that I be given some food.

During that Sunday afternoon the 'crowd from the Castle' took over the Garda station and let the local Gardaí off to attend a football or hurling game. That left the way clear for them to get me alone, without any local interference. My interrogation continued, becoming even more threatening and severe. In one session I was made to stand in front of a desk, behind which sat a detective who continued the abusive interrogation incessantly. Another detective prowled around behind my back and often punched me in the kidneys or jammed his pistol into the kidney area. He would sometimes stamp on my toes or scrape the edge of his shoes down my shin bones. They were all the time cursing, swearing, telling me they would hang me and calling me derogatory names. They told me the locals were off duty and they were in control. They could do whatever they wanted to me, and nobody would ever know.

Eventually, in an effort to get some respite I asked to use the toilet. They refused me permission. I asked several times, only to receive more punches and abuse. After half and hour or so I told them that if they would not let me use the toilet I would piss on the office floor. This really incensed them. After more abuse they stormed out of the room and were replaced by two other detectives. I knew one of them to be a Special Branch man. A short time later the door opened and they were told to take me to the toilet. I was in front, followed closely by the Branch man and the other detective. As we turned down a corridor to the toilet I could see an open door out to the station yard and the street beyond. There was nobody between me and that open door. As I came level with an alcove on the right I saw a bunch of armed detectives standing there. One of them tried to trip me. I stepped over his foot and the Branch man behind me laughed, saying, 'You won't catch Peter that easily.'

Then immediately I heard an angry, excited voice, almost in a scream, yelling, 'I'll fix the bastard! I'll blow his fucking head off, the dirty fuckin' bastard!' And simultaneously I heard him cock his Uzi sub-machine gun. I got an unmerciful shove in my back, propelling me through the toilet door on the left and up against the wall inside. The Branch man spreadeagled across my back, whispering urgently into my ear, 'Say nothing! Say nothing!' and then, shouting to his companion, 'Shut the fucking door!'

As this was happening I could hear shouting, screaming and scuffling in the corridor, and then an authoritative voice demanding, 'What's going on here? Give me that weapon!' And after a slight pause, in a very loud voice, 'Now!' Then the same voice, only a little quieter, told someone to unload the weapon. He then ordered the angry one to go to his office and wait for him there.

After a minute or so, with the Branch man still protecting me, the door opened and someone asked if we were alright. With that the tension left us, and the Branch man laughed, saying, 'I need to have a piss myself now, after all that excitement.'

The three of us laughed in relief. And when I thanked them they just shrugged it off. But I was very grateful to that Branch man for saving my life. I relieved myself, and was allowed to wash my hands and face. The cold water felt so refreshing. They gave me a cigarette, and we had a smoke before they took me back to the interrogation room.

During one of the interrogation sessions there were three detectives with me. Two of them spoke of trying to beat a confession out of me. The third detective, who was the senior one, told them to stop.

'I know Peter,' he said. 'He is not going to say anything no matter how much he is beaten.' He then turned to me. 'I don't think you had anything to do with this, Peter. It's not your style. But make no mistake, if I thought you did it and I could get a confession out of you, I would kick your bollix in, I really would.' He went on, 'I don't think you did this. But the bosses upstairs really want you. You must have done something to make them want you this much.'

Later that night I was taken to another office in the building. As I passed through the same alcove a detective tried to head-butt me. But I was in a state of hypertension and managed to draw my head back, so the blow to my nose was not as bad as it might have been. When I got to the office upstairs, which was that of a superintendent, my nose was bleeding. Seeing a box of tissues on the desk I took some, and held them to my nose to stem the bleeding. A detective was present, and when he saw the blood he grabbed the bloody tissues, chortling, 'We have you now, you bastard. This will fix you.' He put the bloody tissues in an envelope and called out the door to a waiting colleague. He then wrote on the envelope and passed it out the door with instructions to get it to the lab. I had no idea what that was all about. But then, the whole episode was surreal to me.

They tried continuously to get me to say that I had committed the crimes, or to say I was involved in committing them. They used every tactic possible to achieve that, from abusing me, to vilifying Eva and my family, including my Dad, a former Garda. I said absolutely nothing. And as the booze effects wore off I began to feel stronger within myself, even as I was exhausted.

From what they told me I learned that Detective Garda John Morley and Garda Henry Byrne had been killed. I understood how my interrogators were incensed over the loss of their colleagues, but at the time I was unable to feel sorry for the dead men. All I could feel was my own terrible weariness as the interrogations went on and on. I genuinely feared that I might not leave the barracks alive, even though they must have known that I had nothing whatever to do with the crimes. They had to release me by 3 p.m. on Monday, when the 48-hour detention was over. That was the law. I continued to maintain my silence. It was like going through a pain barrier. I did not then consider that they might actually charge me with those crimes. At 4.30 a.m. the next morning they finished interrogating me and put me back in the same stinking cell.

What they were putting me through was like something out of Kafka. The break from the constant harassment was a relief, and I dozed fitfully. They came for me again three and a half hours later. They took me to another room, and interrogation resumed at 8.30 a.m. I had a visit from my solicitor about an hour later. As always, I gave him an account of what was happening to me, and he advised me to continue to maintain my silence. At noon they told me I was to be charged with capital murder and robbery. I was taken directly, under armed escort, to the Special Criminal Court in Dublin. On arrival I was put in a basement holding cell before being brought up to the court via a winding staircase, which entered directly into the dock. During the brief appearance I had intended to complain about my treatment over the last two days. I looked about the court, crowded with police, and said nothing. Fuck it, I thought, I might as well complain to a pack of dogs that one of them had bitten me. I was granted free legal aid and remanded in custody, to appear again on Wednesday, two days later. Hustled into a minibus, crowded with Gardaí and jailors, I was handcuffed to one of them. Escorted by army jeeps, a Special Branch car and motorcycle outriders, I was driven at speed to Mountjoy Prison, where we sat in the minibus for about half an hour. Eventually the convoy sped out of Mountjoy and the city, through the countryside and on to Portlaoise Prison, about 50 miles to the south in the midlands. I don't think I was ever as tired in my life.

11

Portlaoise Prison, or 'the bog' as it was sometimes called, was the top security prison in the state at that time. Provisional IRA, INLA and other political prisoners, deemed by the state to be 'subversive', were held there. The state, by that time, did not recognise any prisoners as 'political'.

About two hours after leaving the court the minibus passed through two gates, stopping before the main gate of the prison. I was taken, still handcuffed to the jailer, to the wicket-door set in the main gate. The bell was rung and we were observed through a viewing slot before the door opened, and we entered the main gate tower. The inner door was not opened until the outer door was locked securely. Through the inner door, we were in a yard. Then we had to be passed through another gate before walking down a laneway to a solid door. This was opened to admit us into a more enclosed space, with a small building on either side. We went in to the one on the left, and my handcuffs were removed. There were four jailers there, including a chief and assistant chief.

I was strip-searched and told to dress in prison clothes, but considering myself to be a political prisoner, I refused. They insisted. I told them I would either wear my own clothes or go naked. As a political prisoner I was not going to wear prison clothes. I was not sure if they would accept my position or try to force me. I was too tired to fight, but at the same time I would not give in. They looked at each other and then at the chief. He shrugged and indicated my clothes, and the tension eased. I was allowed wear my clothes, which were actually the clothes given to me by the police. But at least they weren't prison clothes. This is what is referred to as 'reception'.

I was to be held on E1, the ground floor of a four-storey Victorian, concrete-built prison wing, faced on the outside with stone. At that time the upper three landings – E2, E3 and E4 – housed Provos (Provisional IRA, Provisional Sinn Féin). Being the largest and most disciplined group in the prison, they were also the most powerful. E1 housed 'IRSP' (INLA, IRSP) as well as political prisoners who were not aligned with any particular organisation. I fitted into the latter category.

About 7 p.m. I was escorted to E Wing and locked in a cell on the ground floor. My court appearance had been reported on the evening news, and the prisoners were expecting me. Colm, a prisoner who later became a friend, came to my door to speak to me through the 'Judas hole', as the observation hole was called. He reassured me that I would be allowed out on the landing the following morning. The E1 prisoners had held a meeting and decided I was acceptable to them. I had been in the IRA before the Provos or the other groups were even thought of, and my republican credentials were sound. Some Provos referred to prisoners on E1 as 'mavericks'. Then he asked if I needed anything, and passed me in some cigarettes and matches, for which I was very grateful. At least the cell was clean, and the bedding fresh. I made up the bed, undressed and got between the sheets. Almost instantly I fell into a deep sleep. It was the first real sleep since my arrest on Saturday, and probably my first proper sleep since my drinking binge fourteen days earlier.

I was awakened by a loud screaming outside the cell window. 'Jesus! ... Oh Jesus! ... Please take me! ... Take me Jesus!' There was someone running about the prison yard, with other men running trying to catch him and calm him down. Bloody hell, I wondered, what sort of place is this? He sounded demented, crying, sobbing and screaming as they took him away.

I slept again until the doors opened at 8.30 a.m., when I was able to go out onto the landing and slop out. Portlaoise Prison did not have toilet or washing facilities in the cells. Prisoners were provided with a plastic potty, as used when toilet-training young children. There were toilet cubicles and taps at the end of the wing, where the potty could be emptied and rinsed. These were separate to the toilets and wash basins, also at the end of the wing, used for personal hygiene by the prisoners.

I met and spoke briefly to Pat McCann and Colm O'Shea on the landing. They had also been charged with the same offences as me. I knew Pat, having met him in various pubs in Galway and Dublin. But I had only met Colm briefly on one occasion when he was in Pat's company. I had hardly spoken with him and knew him only to that brief extent. There was no discussion about our common difficulty. I was greeted by a number of other prisoners in E Wing who knew me. I learned then it was a jailor who had gone demented. I was relieved it wasn't a prisoner.

We had what was known as association on the landing until 10 a.m. During this time we could have breakfast, consisting of porridge, tea and bread and butter. At 10 a.m. we had the choice of going for exercise to the prison yard, staying locked in our cells, going to the recreation hall (TV), or going to the woodwork shop. Once in either of these places we had to remain there until 'changeover' at 11 a.m. or 12.30 p.m., when we had to be back on the landing for dinner.

Dinners were placed in what were called 'cookie-wagons', which were mobile, stainless steel, keep-hot cabinets. When we arrived back on the landing we could take a dinner from the cookie-wagon. With less than fifteen minutes to spare before lockup we could eat with neighbours in a cell or retire to our own cell and eat alone. Most of the prisoners chose the former, but I came to prefer eating alone in my cell, which sometimes meant I would be locked in before 12.45 p.m., the official lockup time.

The cells were opened again about 2.10 p.m. We could then avail of the same choices as during the morning, until 4 p.m. when we had to return to the landing for 'tea', which might be a hard-boiled egg and some soggy chips, plus tea, bread and butter. We were then locked up from 4.10 p.m. until 5.30 p.m., when the cells were opened and post was distributed. We could then have association, as during the morning. Supper time was just before the 8.30 p.m. lockup. We were then locked in our individual cells until 8.30 a.m. the following morning.

Being locked in a cell for twelve hours is like being entombed. It is a very daunting experience, which some people handle better than others. Many of the prisoners hated being locked up alone. Some would play their radio at the highest volume, others would climb up to their window and call out to their friends. They would do anything to connect to someone outside their solitude. I was fortunate in that respect; after the hustle and bustle of the prison during the day I was glad to be alone. I looked on my cell as a place of peace and solitude, my sanctuary almost.

On 23 July 1980, two days after I was remanded to Portlaoise, I was taken with Pat and Colm to the Special Criminal Court in Dublin, where the three of us were, joined in one indictment, charged with capital murder and robbery. We were remanded in custody to appear again on 6 October. At that time the Special Criminal Court could not remand directly to Portlaoise. This meant we had to be taken to Mountjoy Prison in Dublin, held briefly in the prison minibus and then moved back to Portlaoise. As a prisoner on remand awaiting trial I was, in law, deemed 'innocent until proven guilty'. As such, under prison rules, I was not supposed to be held in custody with sentenced prisoners. But, such niceties were not applied by the state in my case.

A few days after my arrival back in the prison, one of the teeth which had been built by the dentist in Galway disintegrated, and the second tooth fell apart later that same day. But then the dentist had warned not to get any blows for a couple of months to allow them to harden fully. My enquiries regarding dental treatment within the prison convinced me to wait until I was acquitted and released before attempting to get proper dental treatment. My feet, and toes in particular, were painful as a result of having been stamped on during my interrogations. One big toe festered, and I had to treat it carefully. I got antiseptic ointment from another prisoner, and it got better after a while. When we were locked in our cells during mealtimes the jailers would go for their meals and the wing was patrolled by Gardaí. Sometimes one or more of them would come to my cell and growl through the Judas hole, 'You'll hang, you bastard!' Other times a noose would be tied in a piece of string and dangle it through the hole into my cell, with similar jeers, or one of them would make a drawing of a man hanging and slip it under my door.

Each prison has attached to it a Prison Visiting Committee, a body of responsible outside citizens appointed to oversee the running of the prison. Eventually I put my name down to see the Portlaoise Visiting Committee. I asked them, in the presence of the prison governor, if harassment by the Gardaí was normal practice in their prison. That put a stop to the affair, and I was better able to relax in my cell.

Having been in prison before, it wasn't such a culture shock being inside again. I understood how the system worked, and could handle that. But my being locked up accused of serious crimes that I had nothing to do with, and facing a possible death sentence, was a different matter. One moment I would be elated, with the thought that I just had to be acquitted. The next I would be low with the contradictory thought that I might be convicted and sentenced to death for crimes I had not committed. I clung to the hope that justice might prevail. But even so, I knew that justice could be a precarious affair, especially in the Special Criminal Court. It was regarded by many as merely a sentencing tribunal rather than a court of justice. My situation was further complicated by the fact that I was still suffering from active binge drinking. I was recovering physically but

I still had a craving for booze, and that took much longer to ease. If only I could escape into a bottle of whiskey, that would be a relief. But deep down inside me I knew that wasn't so. I was captured, in every way possible, with no escape. I just had to persevere.

It took a few months before I got any visits. Getting permission to visit a prisoner in Portlaoise was a slow process. A person had to write to the prison for a visiting application form, then get two passport photos and have them, and the form, signed and stamped at their local Garda station. When the prison had received the required material, the decision was made to either allow or refuse the application. If granted, the applicant was notified and could visit the prisoner. Eva was my most frequent visitor throughout my years in prison. Clarrie visited me once, while I was on remand, and some friends also came to see me from time to time.

I got a message from a journalist telling me that he believed there was a 'cover up' in my case. It suggested that the account given to the media about what had happened at the scene of the shooting was not accurate. I told my solicitor about this, who undertook to follow it up, but I heard nothing further. Even sending me the message was a very brave act by the journalist. To attempt to contact him from the prison would have put him in danger. In any case, at the time I felt I had to be acquitted and that I could follow it up myself when I was released.

I received a copy of the Book of Evidence in late September. It was 800 pages long, and I set about trying to read and understand it. I was shocked to read Garda accounts of my detention and interrogations, which they called 'questioning', and the contents of their statements. I had answered absolutely none of their interrogations. I had only given my name, address and date of birth. I told them I was innocent and would not answer any questions. The only other time I spoke was to ask for my solicitor, or to use the toilet, as the need arose. Otherwise I maintained an absolute silence. I would focus on a point on the wall and keep my gaze there, which infuriated some of my interrogators.

The statements in the Book of Evidence claimed that I had 'voluntarily' given samples of my hair, and made a 'voluntary verbal admission', namely 'I know that you know I was involved but on the advice of my solicitor I am saying nothing and you will have to prove it all the way.' I never said those words, and first became aware of them when I read the Book of Evidence. They also alleged that I had acknowledged that the sweater I was arrested in was the same sweater I had worn on 7 July, the day of the crimes. The truth was that I made no such acknowledgement, and in fact I had found the sweater in Peadar's house one night when I was chilly. Their statements painted a much different picture of my detention than waht I knew to be the reality. The death of the two Gardaí was a terrible tragedy, and the members of the force were naturally enraged that two of their colleagues had been killed. They wanted vengeance. They wanted convictions. They wanted executions. I could feel for the dead Gardaí and their grieving families, but I was not responsible for the tragedy. I had been wrongfully put through the mill by their colleagues, and was now facing being tried, possibly convicted and hanged for something I did not do. My sympathy for the two grieving families was tempered by my situation and the behaviour of the state against me.

I could understand that some of the Gardaí would go to any extreme to get convictions, yet even I was shocked that they would engage in what was, as far as I was concerned, a complete fabrication. There was absolutely no evidence that I had any part in the crimes. It seemed to me that in their fury they needed to satisfy their lust for vengeance, without regard to truth or justice. I am not talking about all the Gardaí. Most of them are decent, honest police officers, and probably believed that I was guilty. But that, however, could not be said of all of them. Why me? I asked myself. I remembered what one of my interrogators said to me in Galway: 'I don't see you doing this. But you must have done something for my bosses to want you so much.' Perhaps my republican background was enough for them. I could only speculate on the reasons why I was accused, and get on with doing the best I could in the situation.

Pat McCann and Colm O'Shea would not discuss the case with me. This was understandable, as each of them was pleading not guilty and hoping to be acquitted. But the Book of Evidence made me so angry at times. I was innocent. There was no evidence other than their fabrications. I could not see how I could be convicted, even by the Special Criminal Court.

Séamus Egan, SC was retained as my senior barrister. I heard at the time that he had a 100 per cent success rate in the Special Criminal Court, which sounded good to me. I found out much later that, having won an acquital in his previous case, mine was actually to be his second case in that particular arena. Later the court decided that in capital cases a defendant was entitled to two senior counsels, and Eoin Fitzsimons, SC was added to my defence team. I had a solicitor, two senior counsels and one junior counsel, which seemed quite impressive at the time.

I spent most of my remand time trying to study the Book of Evidence, walking in the prison yard and reading in my cell at night before bed. I was fortunate that I had no problems sleeping, in fact I slept like a baby most nights. I had a number of visits from my solicitor, who seemed to be working hard on my behalf. Eva told me that he had all his staff studying the Book of Evidence and that he and they were even working weekends on the case. As the weeks passed, the effects of my drinking wore off and I felt better. I still yearned for a drink at times but consoled myself with the idea that when I was acquitted and released I could then have a good session. I told myself that in the interim not having a drink would do me good, almost like I was in training.

As my trial date approached, P.J., a fellow prisoner and cabinet maker, brought me to the woodwork shop. This was a large room with work benches and even a wood-lathe, where prisoners could make crafts. At one end there was a wired off section with a jailer in charge, where the tools were kept. If a prisoner required tools, they were carefully checked out to him and had to be returned before he could leave the workshop. Hammers, saws, wood-chisels, Stanley knives and all kinds of woodworking tools were available, under very strict supervision. P.J. showed me the ropes and convinced me to start woodworking, 'to help take your mind off your case and give your head some relief'. We were allowed to purchase mahogany from the prison – only mahogany, for some strange reason. Working with wood gave me a break from the constant preoccupation with my case, and I was very grateful to P.J. for his help and wisdom. I made a mahogany coffee table.

12

he trial started on 6 October and took twenty-three court days over a period of six weeks. Going to court meant being called around 6.30 a.m., and after slopping out, having a wash and some breakfast, we were taken to reception, where we were strip-searched. Then we would have a long wait for the escort to arrive. Gardaí came from Dublin and soldiers from The Curragh in County Kildare. We were brought, each handcuffed to a jailer, through the various gates and doors to the outside of the main gate and bundled into a minibus. The convoy would speed up the road to Dublin, sirens blaring as we passed through towns and villages. On the outskirts of suburban Dublin we would be picked up by Garda motorcycle outriders, who buzzed around us back and forth like hornets, their sirens continually blaring.

We were always moved in a large convoy. First there was an unmarked Garda Special Branch car and a Garda minibus followed, empty except for the driver, in case the bus we were in broke down or got a puncture. Then there was a jeep filled with armed soldiers. We were next, with another army jeep behind us, and a Garda car took up the rear. The convoy moved at top speed, sirens blaring, outriders stopping traffic to let us pass.

Anticipating our arrival, Green Street would be cordoned off to the public. Our minibus would drive into the yard of the Special Criminal Court, where we would each be hustled into the building, along an underground corridor and into a holding cell below the court. The handcuffs would be removed, and we would wait, sometimes for an hour or more. That cell was always very cold, and we shivered there until the court was ready to deal with us. Then we were brought up a narrow, winding stairway leading directly into the dock, which was comprised of two rows of four seats facing the court. Pat and Colm usually sat in one row with their respective jailers and I sat in the other row with my appointed jailer. There was also an assistant chief and sometimes even a chief jailer present.

Green Street Court is a very old building, with a long history of savagery. Robert Emmet sat in the same dock when he was convicted of treason against 'the Crown' on 19 September 1803 and sentenced to be hanged, drawn and quartered. The following day he was publicly executed in Thomas Street, outside St Catherine's Church. Many other rebels were tried and convicted from that same dock down through the years, including the Invincibles and Fenians. The court was panelled in wood which looked like oak to me, and was rectangular in shape.

At the front of the court was the elevated bench where the tribunal of judges sat looking out, and down, upon everyone else. They entered and exited through a door to the side of their bench. The court registrar sat in front of them, facing the body of the court. In front of him, and slightly lower, sat the solicitors – the defence on the left and the state on the right, all facing the judges. The various barristers were next, again with the defence on the left and the prosecutors on the right. The elevated jury box was on the right, between the bench and the prosecutors' position. It remained empty during our trial, as there was no jury. The witness box was also to the right in front of the jury box and lower. The press sat behind the barristers. Behind the press there was a passageway across the width of the court with glass-panelled doorways on either side, leading out to corridors. Behind the passage was the dock, elevated to about the level of the registrar. This was where I emerged, from the underground passage containing the holding cell. At the back of the dock was a wooden partition. Behind the dock, and at a higher level again, were tiers of seats. This was the public gallery. The defendants sat in the dock, facing the bench. The defence lawyers sat some rows in front, and below, also facing the bench, with their backs to their clients.

Because of the layout of the courtroom, it was virtually impossible for me to speak to, or consult with, my lawyers, or even to get their attention during the trial. I was refused permission to sit beside my solicitor. It was very hard to hear what was being said most of the time, unless voices were raised. It was very frustrating. After a short wait the registrar stood and said in a loud voice, 'All rise.' Everybody stood, and the three members of the court filed in to their seats and sat down, bowing and nodding to the body of the court. Then everyone else sat and the proceedings began.

The trial commenced with all the lawyers introducing themselves, saying who they represented. The state and each of the defendants had two senior counsels, two junior counsels (barristers-at-law, BLs) and a solicitor. Apart from the solicitors they were all dressed in black gowns and wore wigs. The three court members – a High Court judge, a Circuit Court judge and a District Court judge – were similarly attired. It felt weird sitting in the dock, observing a process getting under way that I had nothing to do with. My name was mentioned the first day, when the charges were read out by the court registrar. The rest of the day passed slowly. Although I tried to listen carefully to everything that was being said, it was difficult to be attentive to matters that seemed obscure and of no significance to me personally.

In front of me and to my right there was the partition, which meant that persons entering the court on that side could not be seen by the judges unless they advanced along the passage beyond the partition. During the trial I observed several police witnesses, standing out of sight of the bench, listening to their colleagues give their evidence. This meant they could go into the witness box and potentially corroborate the same evidence. I raised this improper behaviour one evening in a consultation with my lawyers, who told me there was very little that could be done about it. I asked that they apply to the court to keep witnesses outside the court until they were called to give their evidence. They said it would be no use, as the court would probably refuse the application and such application would only antagonise the court.

I also observed detectives bringing individuals into the court from the right, standing behind the partition and pointing me and/or the other defendants out to them. Then such people went into the witness box as prosecution witnesses. I again drew this impropriety to the attention of my lawyers. The response I got from them was dismissive. My senior counsel said that 'at least we know what they are up to', but again claiming that we must do nothing to antagonise the court, especially when there was no evidence on which I could be convicted.

The state claimed that two days after the crimes one of the culprits was stopped and questioned, but that he ran away and eluded the chasing Garda. It was claimed that the culprit was me. That very same Garda gave evidence. When he was asked if he would recognise the man again, and if he had seen him since, he asserted that he could definitely identify him and that the man was in the court. Pointing to a man standing at the back of the public gallery, he positively identified him as the man he had stopped and tried to apprehend, saying on oath, 'I see him standing up there with his back against the panel – I would say it is the third row. Up there, I see him up there.' I was sitting in the dock!

Séamus Egan, my senior counsel, who had not even turned to see who the Garda had pointed to, stood to cross-examine, saying, 'You think the man you saw is the man up in the dock there?'

'Yes sir.'

Robert Barr, SC for the prosecution, immediately stood and intervened. He told the court that the Garda had been shown photographs of me before the trial. The presiding judge asked the witness if this was true, and he confirmed it was so. Logically, if the

Garda was shown a photo of me before the trial and still identified the man in the public gallery as the culprit, that should have made his evidence even stronger. Nobody even attempted to detain the man in question. And he quietly disappeared from the court. That evening after court I spoke with my lawyers about this. Séamus Egan told me it was a very good development. He was sure that the court could not convict me after that Garda's evidence. The fact of the matter was that it had happened, and they could not ignore it. He convinced me, and I went along with his reading of the situation. I was much heartened going back to prison that evening.

My lawyers decided that, as there was no evidence connecting me to the crimes, I would not give evidence myself. I argued over this with them, in the belief that I had to state my innocence on oath. In October 1979, the year before, I had actually returned money to a bank after it had made a mistake and given me too much. I felt that this fact would show that I was not a thief or robber. But my lawyers reckoned it was not important, and we would not be allowed enter such evidence anyway.

In a jury trial the jury finds on issues of fact and the judge finds on issues of law. When an issue of law is to be decided, the jury must retire while the issue is argued and decided in their absence. The Special Criminal Court, being a non-jury court, is both a tribunal of law and of fact. Issue arose as to the lawfulness of allowing the verbal statement alleged to have been made by me into evidence. It had to be argued and ruled upon. This would be done in what the court called 'a trial within a trial'. In essence this meant, contrary to what would be allowed in a jury trial, that the tribunal of fact would hear the matter of law being decided and then decide the matter as well.

I was to go into evidence in the 'trial within a trial'. I had told my lawyers about the ill-treatment during my detention, but they insisted that I must not refer to that in the witness box. They pointed out to me that I could not prove that I was ill-treated or that I had been bleeding. It would be my word against the police, and the court would believe the police. My lawyers emphasised that they were the experts, and that I must trust them and only do what they said. I was instructed to answer the questions as briefly as I could and not to elaborate; otherwise the court would get angry with me. We were doing so well, we must not antagonise the court. I did as I was told. The questioning stopped without even asking me if I had spoken the words alleged against me. Before I knew it I was out of the witness box and back in the dock. It was a weird and surreal experience. My solicitor gave evidence of his visits with me while I was detained. The court retired to consider its decision, and when it sat again it allowed the alleged verbal statement into evidence against me.

The prosecution maintained that wool fibres, allegedly found in the getaway car used by the raiders, matched wool fibres taken from the sweater I was wearing when arrested. This was the sweater I had found in Peader's house, when I was staying there after the date when the crimes were committed. They relied on the evidence of a state forensic scientist who claimed that he had established this match by a scientific process called 'Thin Layer Chromotography.' What I didn't know at the time was that Thin Layer Chromotography couldn't conclusively prove a match between fibres, but I did know that the fibres could not have come from the sweater I was wearing when arrested.

Going up and back from court each day was very exhausting. I was strip-searched before leaving the prison and on my return, and the journey to and from the court was long and uncomfortable, not to mention the long periods of waiting in the cold holding cell in Green Street. These journeys were conducted in a very serious fashion, but even so were not without their lighter moments. On one trip, as we were leaving Kildare town towards the prison, we were caught in a line of traffic moving at about 15 miles an hour. The road was narrow, and there was a bad bridge and heavy traffic coming towards us. Despite the sirens, horns and flashing lights, we had to stay in line for about 2 miles. When we eventually got to the head of the line of traffic there was an elderly farmer driving an old tractor and trailer, puffing his pipe contently. The convoy raced past him, sirens blaring, horns blowing and angry Gardaí shaking their fists at him. He smiled and waved to us as we passed, totally unfazed by all the commotion.

The trial ended on 26 November and the court retired to consider its verdict. As it was getting late, the court decided it would give its verdict the following afternoon. Mr. Egan told me this was good as it meant that the court would sit through the night considering the evidence. I heard later that the presiding Judge Hamilton was drinking in a Dublin hotel that night.

The following day, 27 November 1980, Pat McCann, Colm O'Shea and I were brought to the court to hear the verdict. Once again we went up the spiral stairway into the dock and seated ourselves. 'All rise,' the registrar called out, and the three members of the court entered, performing the usual formalities. The presiding member read out the judgement of the court: 'Guilty' against all three of us.

I felt myself withdrawing within myself in shock and disbelief. Even though it was said that this was merely a sentencing tribunal, up until that moment I did not believe it could convict me.

I was convicted solely upon the basis of the oral statement I was alleged to have spoken after forty-three hours' detention and interrogation: 'I know that you know I was involved but on the advice of my solicitor I am saying nothing and you will have to prove it all the way.' I did not say those words. In relation to the wool fibres, the court found that it was not established that they came from the sweater.

Judge Hamilton, the presiding member of the court, handed down the sentences one by one, first Colm O'Shea and then Pat McCann. Addressing me he said:

'Peter Pringle, for the crime of capital murder, that is to say the murder of a member of the Garda Síochána acting in the course of his duty, the law prescribes only one penalty, and that penalty is death. It is therefore the duty of this court to pronounce this sentence.

The court accordingly orders and directs that you Peter Pringle be now removed from this court to the prison in which you were last confined and that you be there detained in custody and on the 19th day of December 1980 you there suffer death by execution in the manner prescribed by law and that after such sentence shall have been carried into effect your body be buried within the precincts of the said prison.

In respect of Peter Pringle the Director of Public Prosecutions has, through his counsel, requested the court to pass sentence in respect of the other charge in which you have been found guilty and which appears on the indictment. In this respect the court sentences you to fifteen years' imprisonment.'

We were not asked if any of us wished to say anything before or after the sentences were passed. My anger was such that maybe it was just as well. We were taken from the court down the spiral stairway and into the holding cell.

After a short time my legal team, without Séamus Egan, arrived to see me. I was taken from the cell to an alcove where they were waiting, and a few minutes later Séamus Egan arrived. When he came up to me, he started to cry. Despite my anger, I found myself standing with my arms around his shoulders, consoling him as he sobbed. Even as this was happening, I reflected that here I was, sentenced to death for a crime I did not commit, consoling my senior defence lawyer who had failed to have me acquitted! At that time I truly felt sorry for him. I believed he knew I was innocent and was devastated by his own failure to win the case. He assured me that we would win our appeal, and I had no option but to go along with that.

As we were being brought to the waiting minibus, and all along the journey, it was obvious that the Gardaí were elated with the outcome of the trial. I heard later that Connolly was toasted by his detective colleagues in a pub near the court. Numbed by what had happened, I sat in silence on the journey back to the prison.

13

Reception into the prison was different now that we were sentenced to death. We went through the usual strip-search, before each of us was examined by the prison doctor. This was my first medical examination since my arrest four months earlier. It took being sentenced to death to get a medical examination in this prison.

We were then taken to an isolated area 'behind the gates'. This was the area where prisoners were put in isolation on punishment, locked up twenty-three hours a day with one hour of exercise in the prison yard in isolation from other prisoners. There were five or six cells 'behind the gates'. My things had already been transferred from my previous cell to this area, and I moved my few belongings in to one of the cells.

It was weird being a condemned prisoner and being behind the gates. I was very angry and shocked that the court had convicted me when I was innocent. A part of me knew the Special Criminal Court could do that but another part did not expect it would happen to me.

We were given some food, and then Chief Stack, the most senior jailer, arrived with some cardboard boxes in his arms. He put these on the table outside the cells on the landing and called us over, as if they were some sort of gift. To my surprise they were children's games, like Ludo and Snakes and Ladders. Stack was probably the most detested official in the prison, but on this occasion he smiled and told each of us that we had his permission to play these games, even with his officers. At first I thought this was some kind of macabre joke but then I realised that he was serious. All I could do was laugh at the absurdity of it all and somehow this last nonsense fitted into a day of total absurdity.

At lockup time they insisted that two jailers spend the night in each of our cells. I was the only one who protested. Stack was sent for and I was told I could either go into the cell or be put into it, but the two jailers must be in my presence at all times, as I was a condemned prisoner. Even in my anger I knew I could not win, so I decided to give in, for that night anyway. Now this was a single cell, about 12 feet by 7 feet with a single army-type bed, a small table and a stool. The electric light was set in to the wall above the solid steel door. Two chairs had been added for the jailers to sit on. There was no toilet or wash basin in the cell and my only toilet facility was a plastic potty.

I was so exhausted that I stripped off and went to bed. The two jailers locked in with me wanted the light left on. They kept talking to each other and moving about. I realised they were nervous being locked up with me as they did not know how to cope with this new situation. Another unforeseen factor was that the jailers were entitled to regular breaks on night shift, requiring the cell door to be clanged open, replacements take their place and the door clanged shut again. The whole procedure was then repeated when they came back from their break. It was impossible to sleep or even to rest. I thought carefully about my options and decided on a plan. From my bed I announced that I wanted to speak to them and that they should listen carefully. They sat up straight. 'I have been told by Chief Stack that as a condemned prisoner I can choose whichever jailers I want to spend the nights with me. If you do not remain quiet enough so that I can sleep I will ask for you to be with me every night.' By the looks on their faces I could see how this horrified each of them. Chuckling to myself at my invention about Stack, I managed to sleep, waking several times and noticing that one of them had his baton out and at the ready. They stayed quiet for the rest of the night.

The next day I protested to the governor. I told him my situation was intolerable and, unless they wanted to fight me each evening and chain me to the bed each night, they would have to improve the conditions. At lockup time that evening we were moved to a large cell on E1 landing. This cell, about 35 feet by 10 feet, had been previously made by knocking four single cells into one for use as a recreation cell. They carried our three beds and belongings from behind the gates and we each chose where they should go. I put my bed in a corner along the end wall farthest from the door. Pat and Colm had their beds placed against the side wall jutting out into the cell. There was a Perspex observation hatch set in the wall just beyond the foot of my bed, with two jailers stationed in the cell next door watching into our condemned cell. There were also five jailers seated just inside the door at the other end of the cell. The rule was two jailers for each condemned man plus a spare jailer to allow for breaks. That was the situation. We were kept behind the gates during the day and spent each night in that bigger cell. The beds had to be moved back and forth twice each day.

The acoustics where we were held were strange. Because the jailers in the observation cell at the foot of my bed had to keep the hatch open to overhear conversations from the death cell, we could clearly hear every sound from the observation cell as well. On one occasion I heard three jailers discussing my execution and whether they would be asked to participate in my hanging. Would they be ordered to participate or would they be asked to volunteer for the job? Would they be paid extra wages, or get a bonus, and/or get time off work? And they discussed what such participation might entail and came to the conclusion that they would have to pull on my legs when I dropped through the trapdoor of the gallows, to make sure my neck was broken. This discussion was conducted in my sight and hearing as if I did not exist. It was as if my humanity was no longer an issue – I was not a person any more to them.

The prison doctor visited each of us nearly every day. One day I was in my cell when he arrived and I offered him a cup of instant coffee. He sat and we talked awhile and this became a routine. He was in his sixties, a widower, and was quite a lonely man who seemed to have little purpose to his life apart from his job. I listened to his troubles and he told me how much he enjoyed our conversations, which had a wide range and seldom touched on the prison. I came to enjoy his visits as well. He asked me if there was anything he could get for me and when I said how I missed not having brown bread he introduced it into our diet. Only once did we discuss my possible execution and when I told him that he would have to be present he was very upset and told me that he prayed it would not happen. After about two weeks we were moved full time into the bigger cell and his visits ended.

Once we were fully moved into the larger cell the windows were blocked off so there was no natural light. There was a TV on a high shelf in the corner opposite the door and this caused a lot of trouble as the jailers wanted to watch the soaps and we did not and often wanted it switched off altogether. The fluorescent overhead lights were on day and night so there was no privacy. There were no toilet facilities or wash-hand basin in the cell and each prisoner had his issue potty. Again I was the only prisoner to protest about this. I told them that if they would not provide me with proper toilet facilities I would piss and shit in the waste bucket which stood beside where the jailers sat inside the door. This threat from me was taken seriously and they had to escort me to the toilet on the landing whenever I asked them. The new arrangement also applied to Pat and Colm.

It was still very difficult to sleep. The jailers shuffled on their chairs, chatting, rustling newspapers and sometimes dozing off and knocking over their chair. Then, of course, each of them had to be relieved for their breaks and for toilet purposes. This meant that they would make a call on a radio, which crackled, and the noisy metal door had to be opened and shut to let them out and again to let them back in. All of this added to my anger and frustration as I faced the imminent threat of execution for a crime I did not commit. I spoke to the doctor and was supplied with ear plugs, which helped a little.

The state wanted to keep condemned prisoners healthy until it executed them. And they did everything they could to prevent a condemned prisoner committing suicide, hence the two jailers assigned to each condemned prisoner. Having sentenced a person to death, the state reserved the power of life and death to itself.

We who were under sentence of death were not allowed to associate with or speak to other prisoners. Our exercise periods were 9 a.m. to 10 a.m., 12.45 p.m. to 2 p.m. and 4.30 p.m. to 5.30 p.m. when other prisoners were locked up for meals. I was the only one who utilised the 9 a.m. to 10 a.m. period and I really enjoyed that hour walking alone. My two 'shadows' would quickly get tired walking after me and stand at the top of the yard. I simply ignored them. Even though it was against the rules, some prisoners would come to their window to talk with me when I was in the 'Provo' yard. Frankie from County Tyrone spoke with me regularly and kept me up to date with news from the rest of the prison. He was very witty and fearless and if my shadows came close to even try to listen to our conversation he would berate them heartily, right down to their 'seed, breed and generation'. For me, in my situation, Frankie was like a breath of fresh air and I looked forward to our talks.

The prison management were paranoid about security. Every time we went out to the yard on exercise the cell was searched, even though we were never out of the jailers sight day or night. This was the period of the hunger strikes in the H Blocks in the North. One day, when we returned to the cell from exercise, I found that someone had written 'Fuck you and fuck them' across the bottom of my H Blocks poster. It could only have been a jailer.

At the time I said nothing. But when the Visiting Committee next came to the prison I asked to see them. In the presence of the governor and his deputy I told the committee about it and about how some jailer had written 'Death Cell' over the door to our cell. They expressed doubt that such things could happen, especially when the governor stated that none of his officers would do such a thing. When the deputy governor went to slip from the room I asked the chairman of the committee to prevent him doing so and invited the committee to come and investigate the matter immediately before prison staff could do a cover-up. I was returned to the cell and soon afterwards some of the committee arrived and saw that I had told the truth. The deputy asked me for the poster and I refused to give it to him. When I returned from our next exercise period the offending part of the poster had been cut off and removed. I heard later that management sought handwriting samples from the jailers on duty in our cell the day the poster had been defaced.

One day a jailer passed an envelope to me. 'From the chaplain,' he said. I opened it to find a short handwritten note that had been sent to the prison chaplain asking him to 'pass on the three enclosed scapulars to the three condemned prisoners'. These are Catholic religious items – two pieces of square material joined by two strings attached to corners. The idea was that one would wear it over the shoulders, one square to the front and one square to the back. One put it on by putting one's head through the opening between the two cords. I laughed at the idea and gave them to Pat and Colm, but on consideration I realised that even if it was from a religious crank, the person had thought of us and that was what mattered. The prison chaplain, who did not bother to deliver it to us himself, did not visit me at all while I was under sentence of death.

An American friend applied to visit me, and when her passport photos were presented to the Gardaí, she was asked, 'Why do you want to visit that bastard?' She was then told that if she persisted with going to visit me she would not get her residency visa renewed.

Not many people applied to visit condemned prisoners because emotionally it was very difficult. And if they did apply they were made to feel threatened. My friend Eva successfully navigated the difficulties, although continually harassed. A few other friends persisted likewise.

When called for a visit I was escorted to the visiting area where I was strip-searched. I refused to remove my clothing and they had to strip me naked while I stood rigid in the middle of the room. Then when ordered to bend over I would hold myself stiffly upright as they struggled to bend me in order to complete the inspection. After a while they would just say, 'Ah, fuck him' and I would get dressed and go on my visit. The whole thing was crazy. I was watched twenty-four hours a day, every day, by at least two jailers. What could I be attempting to smuggle out through a visit? Ludo pieces in my arse?

Visits were 25-30 minutes long. They were held in a wooden hut which was divided along its length (about 12 feet) by a counter with two fine mesh fences about 15 inches apart from counter to ceiling along the middle. The jailer sat at one end so he could see between the wire fences and also both the prisoner and visitor on either side. He could hear every word spoken. Prisoners were not allowed to describe conditions or talk about the prison on threat of having the visit stopped. This made visits very difficult as naturally visitors wanted to know how I was coping and what I had to cope with. While it was good to see friends from the outside world, visits were a mixture of warmth towards my visitors and anger and frustration with the awfulness of the conditions. Visitors were searched on their way in as well, but usually not strip-searched. After the visit I was put through the strip-search procedure again before being escorted back to the condemned cell.

Eva made representations on my behalf to various TDs (members of parliament), to try to improve the conditions, to little avail. Dr Noël Browne and his colleague Eileen Desmond were the only public representatives who showed any interest in our welfare.

A few weeks later, through the good offices of Dr Noël Browne, TD and my solicitor, I was told that the visiting barrier would be removed. And it was, only to be immediately replaced by a Perspex wall, which was worse. This made it almost impossible to have a conversation between prisoner and visitor. The jailer still sat in his wire cage. Rather than shout through the solid barrier, Eva and I opted to stand on opposite sides of this cage and converse over his head. I went to see the governor about this, who told me he was acting on orders from the Minister for Justice and the matter was out of his hands. I later learned that the minister had in fact ordered the removal of the barrier and that the governor had put up the Perspex wall on his own initiative. Visiting conditions continued in this way for my entire time under sentence of death.

After a couple of months Peter Rogers, a Provo, was sentenced to death and this created an interesting situation. Ours was the only death cell in the prison and the Provos would not mix with non-Provo prisoners. Their OC got permission to speak to us and we were asked if we would agree to Peter sharing our facilities, such as they were. We had no objection and readily agreed, even though this would further cramp our already limited space. Peter was moved in to our cell and then there were four prisoners and nine jailers in a space designated originally for four prisoners. His addition to our restricted little world livened things up as Peter was quite gregarious.

In Ireland, condemned prisoners were entitled to two bottles of stout per day, for 'health reasons'. When I was offered the two bottles of stout I became very angry and refused them in the certain knowledge that two bottles of stout would only create a terrible thirst in me and make me miserable. I gave my stout allotment to Pat and Colm to share between them. Had I been offered two bottles of whiskey I would have gladly accepted them. After Peter joined us they would often stockpile the booze for a day or two and then have a bash, which was funny at times as they got merry quickly. I tried to distance myself from such antics and often lay on my bed with my eyes closed, daydreaming or trying to meditate.

Christmas 1980, spent in the condemned cell in Portlaoise Prison, was not a happy time for me. Hearing Christmas songs and carols and the media focus on spending on presents and having a happy Christmas increased my feelings of loneliness and loss and isolation from the outside world. Fearful of how things might be for my children and being unable to see them or be with them tore me up inside and I felt forlorn and broken-hearted. Each of them made a special Christmas card for me. Receiving those wonderful gifts filled my heart to bursting point even as the pain within me was unbearable. I had to keep my feelings to myself and pretend that I was alright. There was really no one I could have shared with anyway.

The food improved for Christmas Day. With their Guinness rations saved for a few days my three condemned companions tried to create a party atmosphere in the condemned cell and we all made light of our situation, on the surface anyway. I went on my walks in the yard as usual and was enlivened somewhat by my chats with Frankie. Those brief interludes out under the sky were the highlight of my Christmas. And walking alone in the prison yard I could weep silently, releasing a little of my pain.

Shortly after Christmas I received a card from a woman whom I did not know, telling me that she had been walking on the shore at Greystones (County Wicklow) grieving over the loss of her brother Peter. He had been a seaman who lost his life in an accident aboard his ship. She said that she remembered there was another Peter, also a seaman, who was under sentence of death and she decided to send him a card wishing him well. I visualised this woman walking alone on the sea shore mourning for her lost brother and I felt for her in her grief. Receiving her card lifted my heart and spirit enormously. I remain forever grateful to her for her thoughtfulness and generosity of spirit, whoever she may be.

Even so, my heart was heavy over how I had lost contact with my children and my inability to communicate meaningfully with them. I was allowed to write out of the prison but in those letters was not allowed to talk about the prison. I was also very aware that every letter in or out of the prison was censored and my pride would not allow me expose my inner self to prison staff. And I was so filled with remorse, shame and sadness over my boozing and being separated from my children that I found it impossible to write properly to them.

I applied for a welfare visit with my family before my execution date and was told to apply to see the welfare officer. I put my name down to see him and was brought to an office where he sat behind a table. He said, 'What can I do for you?' I told him I was applying for a welfare visit with my family, to which he replied, 'Why?' I told him that I was under sentence of death and he said, 'Why do you want a welfare visit?' He sat there blank-faced and I wondered if he really did not understand or was being deliberately obtuse. I could feel my anger rising and sought to control myself.

I took a deep breath and again told him my circumstances and as a prisoner sentenced to death I wanted a proper welfare visit with my family and again he asked me, 'Why?' At this I said, 'It is obviously a waste of time and effort trying to talk with you,' and I stormed out of the office before he could provoke me more and I could be convicted of a murder I did commit. Back on the landing it took ages for my anger to subside. It was very difficult coming to terms with the coldness of his response to my reasonable request.

Some time later I got a letter from Clarrie telling me that she and the children were coming for a welfare visit. They were brought to the building at 'reception', opposite where prisoners were strip-searched on entering or leaving the prison. I was strip-searched before and after that visit with my family. The room where the 'welfare' visit was held had a wide counter down its length. This was the same room where we had waited for the escort to the court each morning. Clarrie and our children were placed at one side of this counter, the same welfare officer beside them. I had to sit across the counter. We were forbidden any physical contact. Jailers were outside observing through the window. The visit lasted about thirty minutes. It was awful for me and must have been even more so for my family. We were nervous and did not know what to say to each other. I could not talk about prison or the conditions inside and so our conversation was stilted and unnatural. All I could do was act casual and try to ease their concerns, without being really able to do that properly. They in turn tried to make things easy for me and none of us succeeded. I was shattered afterwards, as were they. All in all it was very unsatisfactory for everyone. For me the worse part of it was that the visit was conducted by the same welfare officer listening to our every word.

Frankie was reported by Stack for talking to me and put on a charge, and as a result he lost two weeks' remission. But that did not stop Frankie and we continued to talk at his window. He got an idea of how to get back at Stack and we put his plan into action. We pre-agreed which toilet I would use the next morning. He wrapped up a turd in a parcel in layers of plastic, each layer taped up, until it was about the size of a wrapped stick of gelignite. Then the following morning during slop out he slipped into that cubicle and deposited the parcel in the toilet cistern.

When I was escorted to the same cubicle I washed and made sure to sit in on the toilet. On my way back to the death cell I passed Frankie standing casually at his cell door. Before any other prisoner would be allowed use the cubicle I had used, it was thoroughly searched and the parcel was discovered in the toilet cistern. Chief Stack was immediately sent for and he personally removed the parcel from the cistern and carried it, held out in front of him carefully, down the length of the landing and out of the block, all the time ordering everyone to stand clear of the danger. We learned later that the parcel was brought to an office in another building. An Army bomb disposal squad was called in and the parcel was carefully investigated, each layer of plastic being gingerly peeled away until the turd was revealed.

Meantime I was in the death cell, propped up on my bed reading the paper. Suddenly Stack burst into the cell, shouting and spluttering red-faced and incensed, pointing at me and yelling at me. 'You! You! You! You were in on it. I know you were. You! You! You!' 'Something bothering you chief?' I replied, smiling. 'Calm down or you might get a stroke or heart attack. What's wrong?' He was in such a tantrum he could only splutter, and he stormed out again, crashing the door shut behind him. Frankie had told the other prisoners the story and when Stack stormed back onto the landing in his tantrum everyone was standing around laughing. Later, when I was out on exercise in the Provo yard, Frankie and I exchanged our versions of events, and that was of course circulated throughout the block to every prisoner's delight.

I often thought of Tomás McCurtain and his account to me of his experiences when he was sentenced to death back in the 1940s. He was held in Mountjoy Prison in the condemned cell, the same one we were using as our recreation cell when I was there. He was alone in that cell except for having two jailers with him all the time. He used to laugh and joke about how dense they could be and the little pranks he'd play on them.

In Ireland in those days executions were not unusual and were carried out at 8 a.m. He wrote his final letters to his loved ones the morning he was scheduled to be hanged and prepared himself to face the gallows. All was quiet in the prison as the appointed time arrived. There was no sound of the hanging party, and at 8.05 a.m. he joked with his jailers that they could not even be in time for his hanging. Just before 8.10 a.m. he heard footsteps along the landing and the cell door opened. He stood ready to face his death. The prison governor entered the cell and told him that his death sentence had been commuted to life imprisonment. That development was relayed to the prison the previous midnight but he was not told until ten minutes after he was due to die.

When he told me all this I said he must have felt great that day having escaped the hangman. But he told me it was the worst day of his life! His every thought, feeling and expectation went no further than 8 a.m. that morning. Then he had to get to grips with a new reality and he just did not know what to do or how to cope. Coming to terms with being alive was incredibly difficult and it took him days to get over the cruelty of it all. Knowing Tomás and knowing his story somehow helped me and gave me strength to face whatever might ensue. It was as if the universe gave me the gift of preparation.

I received a card from another stranger. It had a picture of cattle in a field under a cloudy sky and with the sun shining above the clouds. Its caption read, 'Above the clouds the sun is always shining'. I felt lifted that someone unknown to me would think to send it to me in my death cell.

I continued my practice of meditation every day. Sometimes it was almost impossible to still my mind, but I persevered because deep in myself I sensed that my life depended on my being able to rise above my situation. On one such occasion I had the realisation that all they could do to me was kill me. My only fear then was that I might not be able to die with dignity and I determined that no matter what, I would maintain my inner discipline and not let myself down. This realisation gave me a curious sense of freedom within myself. I knew that while they could keep me physically imprisoned and could put me to death, they could not control my mind or my spirit. Within myself I was as free as a bird. In that spirit and realisation I determined to make the best of whatever time might be left to me in this life, regardless of my circumstances.

A horse named Aldaniti was to be ridden by Bob Champion in the 1981 Aintree Grand National. He had been very ill with cancer and had recovered. The horse had suffered serious injuries and his owner refused to have him put down and had nursed him back to health. Nobody gave them much hope of completing the course, never mind winning the race. I was in credit for £5 with a bookie in Galway and I asked Eva to tell him to put my £5 on Aldaniti to win. I reckoned they suited me in my situation. I was very excited watching the race on TV. The betting odds were 12½ to 1. I was thrilled and delighted seeing them pass the finishing post, winners of the race and winners in life, and saw it as a positive omen for myself.

In April 1981, our Applications for Leave to Appeal were heard before the Court of Criminal Appeal, presided over by Chief Justice O'Higgins. With him sat Judges Finlay and Costello. They were very Right-wing in the Fine Gael mode. That political party in the 1930s spawned Ireland's own fascist organisation known as the Blueshirts, which organised a brigade to go to Spain in support of General Franco. The court reserved its judgement and we were returned to Portlaoise Prison to await the verdict.

On 22 May 1981 we were brought before the Court of Criminal Appeal to hear the court deliver its verdict – refusing each of us our Application for Leave to Appeal. When Judge O'Higgins finished reading the judgement and set a new date for our executions on 8 June 1981 I stood and attempted to address the court. I spoke loudly and clearly, telling them they had made a grave mistake, a mistake which could yet prove to be fatal for me and that I was innocent. As I addressed the court the three judges jumped up and nearly fell over themselves in their scrambled haste to get away. It was quite astonishing to see them push and shove each other in their efforts to disappear, all dignity gone. It would have been hilarious except it was so serious. When I sat down again a young barrister, unknown to me, who had been sitting behind me observing proceedings, reached over to thank me and to sympathise. I was touched and glad of his effort.

There was a strange anomaly about the workings of the Court of Criminal Appeal in my case. My Application for Leave to Appeal was heard by the court, which made an order refusing that application. The media reported that I had an appeal and the accepted wisdom was that my appeal had been refused. In reality I was denied an appeal, as confirmed by the order of the court.

We were returned to the death cell in Portlaoise Prison, with our execution date three weeks away. My lawyers came to see me, telling me the government cabinet had met and could not agree on whether to hang me or not. Séamus Egan in particular was very upset and worried that the government might order my execution. My legal team wanted to enter a plea for clemency on my behalf. I told them that on no account were they to plead for clemency for me. I would not plead for clemency for something I did not do. 'But the cabinet is to meet again to discuss the question of your execution and they just might decide to hang you,' Egan said. 'Well it wouldn't be the first innocent person they have executed,' I replied. I then gave them my written instructions not to enter a plea of clemency on my behalf and they left, looking very depressed.

On 27 May 1981, six months after I was sentenced to death and twelve days before I was due to be hanged, I was brought to the prison governor's office. Without preamble he told me, 'You are now serving forty years' penal servitude without remission.' Somewhat taken aback by his statement, I replied, 'On what authority?

'On my authority,' he asserted.

'I want a copy of such warrant or order,' I demanded.

'You can't have it,' he replied. 'Get your solicitor to apply for a copy.' And with that I was hustled out of his office and back to E Block, amazed that I had just received a sentence of forty years' penal servitude without remission from the prison governor who had no authority or jurisdiction to impose any such sentence upon me. I received no official notification that my death sentence had been commuted or that it had been replaced by forty years' penal servitude without remission. I read about it the following day in the newspapers.

14

When I was brought back to E Block, my bedding and belongings had already been moved out of the death cell into a cell on E1 landing among the general prison population. I now had a cell to myself, and the same facilities as when I was on remand. I enjoyed the extra bit of freedom, being able to mix with other prisoners. And while there were still lots of jailers about I would no longer have my two shadows trailing after me.

That afternoon I went to the yard for exercise and stopped to chat with another prisoner sitting on the bench seat against the prison block. As we talked, two prisoners started to run fast, together, down the length of the yard. At first I thought they were racing each other, but when they reached the other end of the yard they scrambled up to the top of the high-wire gate. They were trying to escape. They got to the top of that first gate only to become entangled in concertina wire. The alarm sirens went off. A soldier on the roof fired a warning shot over their heads, which ricocheted off the outer wall. I pressed in close to the prison block and as far as possible out of the line of fire. I certainly did not want to get shot on my first day out of the death cell.

The yard filled with jailers. The two would-be escapees were taken away and put on punishment. One by one everyone left in the yard was brought back indoors and strip-searched. Then we were locked in our cells, as was everyone else on the landing, until the following morning. That evening each cell was searched, and searched again, and again, with more strip-searches each time. This practice was very upsetting. Bedding and belongings were taken out of the cell. Then everything was thrown back in. When they had finished I would sort out the cell and re-make my bed, but a short time later the whole thing would be repeated, and repeated, again and again. It was not easy to remain calm in the face of this sort of provocation. The following morning the landing returned to its usual routines. The two on punishment would remain in isolation for two months. They also lost two weeks' remission.

Security in Portlaoise Prison was incredibly tight and Willie O'Reilly the governor was obsessed on that score. Whenever he refused a request from a prisoner his answer was 'Security', and that was the end of the matter. Strip-searches and cell searches happened regularly, sometimes several times in the same day. Out walking in the yard, we'd hear the clatter of metal bed frames being thrown out of cells as every cell was searched. And when we'd go in for dinner we'd find that our things had been just thrown back into the cell, all in a proper mess. It was hard to stay cool in the face of such provocation. And not everyone succeeded. So at times there would be fights and skirmishes and even more trouble.

The novelty of being back among the prison population wore off very quickly. The pressure of being in the death cell, and possibly facing being hanged, was gone, but the enormity of the forty-year sentence now hit me. How on earth could I face forty years in this hell hole? I could not get my mind around that reality. The prospect was simply beyond reason to me. I could think of nothing else. Finally I decided to kill myself; I could see no other solution. In keeping with my decision I decided to let Eva go out of my life. When she came to see me I told her to go make a life for herself without me. Just because I was locked up did not mean that her life should be ruined too. She was silent a moment, and then said, 'What's wrong with you? Is it that you cannot face the sentence? You look after yourself in here, and let me decide what I want for my future, and let's say no more about it.'

That night, back in my cell, as I thought over everything I broke down and wept. I then realised that if I killed myself they would say I did so out of guilt and remorse, and that would only add to the already heavy burden on my children. I could not do that. This left me with one remaining option – to try to prove my innocence. Arriving at that decision gave me some purpose. But every time I tried to read up on my case I became so angry. My eyes would water up and I could not even see the print on the pages. Oh, it was so frustrating! And I got lower and lower in myself. One morning, when the cell doors opened, instead of getting out of bed I turned to the wall, pulled the blankets over my head and decided everything was useless. I would just stay in bed. And I gave up. I lay in bed like that for five days, only getting up to use the potty and slop out. Then I realised that feeling sorry for myself was not going to help me. I had to bring myself from feeling negative to feeling positive. I had to find a way into positive actions.

I got out of bed the next morning and scrubbed out my cell. I went to the laundry, which we could use before yard time, and washed my clothes. Then I went to the yard for a walk. During that walk I observed the sky and the direction the clouds were travelling. Seeing the sky and the clouds reconnected me to my life at sea before my arrest. I began to feel better. I decided that if I was to try to prove my innocence I would need to study my case. I would need to study the law relating to my case. I would need to study criminal law in general and I would need to study the Constitution.

That evening in my cell I began to read the transcript of the trial. But I could not do it; it was so frustrating. I gave up and walked the cell up and down, up and down, up and down, ready to burst with rage. As I came up to my steel locker, standing in the corner beside the door, I punched it, punched it and punched it until my knuckles bled and the pain in my hands overcame my rage.

I tried again to study the transcript, and again my anger stopped me. I needed to learn to relax. But how could I learn this? I had heard of yoga and meditation. I had even tried to meditate, although not very successfully. I told Eva of my difficulty. On her next visit she left me a little yoga book that had illustrations of yoga positions, postures and instructions. It was very difficult trying to get my body into yoga positions on my own in my cell whilst holding the book open in one hand so I could see the relevant illustration. Meditation was also difficult to accomplish. I would lie stretched out on the cell floor, close my eyes and try to be still. Only my thoughts kept interfering. The more I tried, the harder it became. But I am a very stubborn person and I persisted. Sometimes all I could do was pace up and down the cell, venting my anger and frustration on that poor old metal locker by the door.

Eventually, through my solicitor, I managed to get a copy of the 'Order of the President' commuting the death sentence. I was surprised to discover that the Order of Commutation, and imposition of the sentence of forty years' penal servitude without remission, was a collective one, naming all three of us. There was no individual Order of Commutation and replacement sentence in relation to Peter Pringle. Such contempt and, as far as I was concerned, abuse of due process was astonishing, even to me.

Slowly but surely I began to get the hang of yoga and meditation. And my anger eased a little. During one of the regular security checks, with nothing in my cell but the mattress, the potty, a flask and my plastic utensils, I stretched out on the floor just to let go, not making any conscious effort. And I arrived into a meditative state of being. It was like magic! Afterwards I felt calm, rested and very clear-headed. That's when I began to understand what was meant by 'do without doing', 'concentrate without concentrating'. My yoga efforts also improved and my anger became much less. I was able to study. It was like a miracle to me.

I was not allowed to have even a copy of the Irish Constitution without a covering letter from a solicitor. Eva worked in the university in Galway where she had access to the Law Library. She would copy statutes and parts of law books for me as I needed them. She arranged with my solicitor Leonard Silke's secretary for a covering letter, and in that way I got them in to the prison. At first I would study in my cell until bedtime, but I discovered that I did not sleep well because my head was full of legal stuff, and so I developed a routine. I'd stop work by 10 p.m., do some light reading before bed, and sleep like a top. Then I'd get up at 6.30 a.m., do some yoga, usually the Salutation to the Sun series of exercises, followed by meditation. I would work on law until the cells were opened at 8.30 a.m., or until they came in to search me and my cell, whichever came first.

Through yoga and meditation my legal studies progressed, and I began to gain a good understanding of how the criminal justice system functioned in Ireland. Sometimes other prisoners would ask me to look at their cases, and this helped me too. I even managed to put cases together for some of them, and they were acquitted or won their appeals.

The prisoners I shared facilities with were a mixed bunch. Some were INLA, and considered themselves, somehow, above the rest of us. Some had been upstairs with the Provos, and had either left them on their own account or had been put off the Provo landings. I think I was the oldest prisoner on E1 at the time. Some had been Provos on the outside but chose not to go with the Provos when they were imprisoned. Some had fallen out with the Provos before they were imprisoned and could not go with them when they came inside. I got along with most of the prisoners. I kept away from schemes and conspiracies, which are the norm of prison life, and distanced myself from the INLA and any of their rules and regulations. Because of my own long political background I was tolerated, and mostly left to my own devices.

Eva continued to visit me and we exchanged regular letters. We had a relationship of sorts, dictated by the situation we were in. Every letter was censored going out or coming in. Even letters from the High Court or the Supreme Court carried the censor's stamp. The most painful thing for me was the distance from my children. Letters between us were often stilted and difficult. I could only write about mundane things and they could not possibly understand the reality of life in prison. I was not allowed to write about the prison and I was unable to write properly about my feelings. We expressed our love and I asked how they were doing at school. Sometimes they sent me photos, which really was a treat, but at the same time heightened my sense of loss and distance from them. They were growing up and finding their own ways in life, and I was stuck in prison away from them and from the world.

Leonard Silke visited me and tried to help me in my case. He spoke to Mary Robinson, SC, who agreed to look into matters. She was a brilliant lawyer, very much opposed to the Special Criminal Court and a stalwart for human rights. She prepared a case for me, challenging the constitutionality of my trial by the Special Criminal Court and the death penalty. In the meantime I had begun to uncover material about my trial, which convinced me that I would only have one shot at winning my case. I decided to try to uncover more and prepare a more comprehensive challenge. When Mary Robinson was later asked to stand as a candidate for the presidency of Ireland she first enquired if I wanted her to take my case to the courts. This illustrated for me her selflessness and integrity. I told Leonard my position, and sent my thanks and good wishes for her success. She was nominated as a candidate and elected as the first woman president of Ireland.

Leonard gave up his criminal practice and it was taken over by his colleague Pádraic Ferry. Pádraic visited me and, together with Paul McDermott, BL tried to help me prepare my case. Paul was a fine young barrister and co-author of Prisoners' Rights Under the Irish

Constitution, an excellent book. I remain very grateful to them for their interest in my situation, especially as they knew I had no money to pay for their services.

I became friends with Tommy, another prisoner, who had a very keen mind and an interest in law. We spent many hours and days discussing how it worked as we walked up and down the prison yard. He helped me a lot in coming to an understanding of how criminal law should work, and how it was worked, in Ireland and in particular in the Special Criminal Court.

As my studies progressed I began to take a more informed look at the details of my case. I was arrested and detained under Section 30 of the Offences Against the State Act, 1939, for the murder of a Garda. I discovered that there was no power of arrest for murder or robbery under the Act. There was no power to detain me under the Act. The Special Criminal Court had jurisdiction to try, convict or acquit a person brought lawfully before it under that same Act. But, as I was arrested for murder and detained under that Act, that meant I had been brought before the court while unlawfully detained. Therefore, I was not brought lawfully before the court and the court did not have jurisdiction to try me, convict me or sentence me under the Act. In a nutshell I was unlawfully in prison. All this as well as the fact that I was innocent.

The implications were enormous. If I was correct it meant that the judges of the trial court either did not properly know the law they were administrating. But what about my lawyers? And the other lawyers in the trial? There were four lawyers to each defendant and four lawyers for the prosecution. That meant that sixteen lawyers, as well as the three members of the court, didn't understand the relevant law properly.

The next time Pádraic Ferry and Paul McDermott came to see me I put the issue to them. But I could not convince them. They believed that Section 30 was being administered correctly. They even convinced me that I was wrong. I returned to my cell, very despondent. I didn't even look at my notes that evening. I read a thriller and went to bed, very low in myself.

The following morning, as usual, I got up at 6.30 a.m. I did my yoga and lay on the floor to meditate. When I came out of my meditation I was refreshed and knew what to do. And I knew that I was correct. I realised that my approach to convincing my lawyer friends was the wrong one. I had argued simply on the statute. I needed to go to the basic law, which is the Irish Constitution. Renewed in my belief, I studied the Constitution and the statute within the provisions of the Constitution.

The next time Pádraic and Paul came to see me I raised the question of Section 30 with them again. I could see the frustration in their faces but asked them to hear me out one more time, and if they were not convinced I would not raise the issue again. They resignedly agreed, and I went through it again, but this time from a constitutional perspective. When I was finished they sat across from me in silence. I could see that they were shocked. They nodded, but then excused themselves and left, wishing me well but saying nothing about what I had laid out for them. I returned to my cell, happy that I had convinced them that I was correct about the misuse of Section 30. But what good would it do me? My former SC, Séamus Egan, was appointed to the High Court. In 1986, six years after my conviction, he heard the Trimbole case, in which he laid down the definitive judgement regarding the correct use of Section 30. This confirmed my belief and understanding. I later learned that Paul McDermott had altered his lecture to young barristers, correcting the misunderstanding of the powers of Section 30. On one level I was heartened by this development, but on another I began to recognise just how difficult it would be for me to get justice in my case.

I couldn't help but think how different it would have been if Séamus Egan had argued at my trial in accordance with his later judgement. I believed Séamus Egan to be an honest man, and I now understood that at the time he and the other lawyers in my case did not comprehend that the Act was being misused. The Gardaí probably did not know either. Somewhere back along the line its misuse had been allowed to creep in and, over time, the malpractice became the practice.

The judges I viewed differently. They were appointed under the Constitution to administer justice and had a responsibility to ensure that a person brought before them for trial was lawfully before them. They had a responsibility to know the law, and to administer it justly.

It was interesting to me that Judge Hamilton was later appointed to be the Chief Justice. One of the senior counsels in the case died. Three were appointed to the High Court and one later became the Attorney General.

When I had been in prison a couple of years I noticed one prisoner beginning to behave a bit strangely. I remarked on this to one of my friends, who said, 'He's becoming institutionalised.' I thought about this and realised that if other prisoners could become institutionalised then it could happen to me as well. I could find no reading material in the library on the subject and finally came to the conclusion that the one person available to me who should know about it was the psychiatrist. To get to see the shrink one first had to go to the doctor, and when I told him that I wished to see the psychiatrist he asked why. I said it was none of his business, unless he was a psychiatrist. A few days later I was called to see the shrink and I asked him to tell me about institutionalisation. I explained that if it could affect other prisoners it could affect me, and I wanted to be able to deal with it. He told me that in all his years' experience I was the first prisoner to ask him about institutionalisation. He explained that it was like coming to a 'psychological fence', using the Grand National as a metaphor. Some people hit the fence early in their sentence, after six months or a year. The big fence usually came between four to six years, and this was like Becher's Brook, with lots of fallers. He asked me to describe how I spent my days in the prison and so I told him about my work, my walks and yoga and meditation. He reckoned that I had already found my own answer to the problem by structuring and varying my days, albeit within the prison confines.

Over four years after my trial I got a letter into the prison from George Ryder of Oceanic Services asking if I had been paid for the trip I had made to Inis Mór with 4,000 concrete blocks on Wednesday 2 July 1980. That was the same date that one of the cars used in the crimes was stolen in Galway. This was very interesting because, during my trial, evidence was allowed regarding the theft of the cars used by the bank raiders. The trial court ruled that the theft of the cars formed part of the *res gestae* of the case. In lay terms, the theft of the cars was an ingredient of the crimes with which we were charged. It follows that whoever stole the cars committed the crimes.

One of the vehicles used as a getaway car was stolen from the car park of a hotel in Galway between 11 p.m. and midnight on Wednesday 2 July 1980. That was the evening I sailed the *Severn Princess* into Kilmurvey Pier on Inis Mór, with 4,000 concrete blocks. When the car was stolen in Galway I was on Inis Mór discharging the concrete blocks – and there were lots of witnesses to that fact. The significance of this did not strike me until I received the letter. It transpired that the client who received delivery of the blocks did not pay for them. When he was threatened with legal action for payment he claimed that he had paid me, which was untrue. When eventually it came to court, the client did not appear and he had to pay up.

I dug my copy of the Book of Evidence from a box under my bed and looked up the statement of evidence in George Ryder's name. According to the statement attributed to him, I had sailed at 11 a.m. and returned to Rossaveal at 11 p.m. If this was true it could possibly have been me who had stolen the car, but the reality was that I was on the Aran Islands at that time and didn't get back to Rossaveal until the early hours of the next day. George had been subpoenaed as a witness for the prosecution at my trial. He was never asked about the sailing times in this oral evidence but it was there in the Book of Evidence. I wrote to him about this and learned that not only did he not make that statement about the sailing times, but that he said he was never even asked about what time I sailed and returned that day. He first learned of the statement he was supposed to have made when I sent him a copy of it. Had he been asked to make a statement about the sailing times, the Oceanic Services log books would have made it clear that I could not have stolen the car in Galway. A statement containing false evidence that he did not give to Gardaí was inserted in the Book of Evidence and attributed to him. I was very grateful for his honesty and courage in making his affidavit. Incidentally, the stolen car was repaired and returned to its owner before the Book of Evidence was served upon me, which meant that my defence could not examine it.

Eva left a portable typewriter and a ream of typing paper in to the prison for me to help me in preparation of my case. When I went to Governor Reilly to ask permission to have them he refused, saying, 'You cannot write to judges.' I explained that my purpose was to prepare my case, which I intended in the future to put before the courts – and also to perhaps do some creative writing. With that, he said, 'Go do your writing. Show it to me, and then I'll consider giving you the typewriter.'

'Ok, let me have the paper so I can do the writing,' I replied, but he refused. I went to him each week with my request, and each week I was refused.

Eventually I went to the doctor and asked to see the psychiatrist. About a week later, as I was about to collect my food at 4 p.m., a jailer approached me. Speaking softly, he told me the doctor wanted to see me. 'Doctor? You mean the shrink?' He was trying to be discreet, and was surprised that I would openly speak of going to see the psychiatrist. I laughed, and he escorted me out of the block to an office where the psychiatrist waited. I insisted on seeing him alone, and the jailer left to wait outside the office door. 'What can I do for you?' the shrink asked. 'I want you to examine me to find out if I am crazy,' I said. 'What makes you think you are crazy?' he asked, to which I replied, 'I don't think I am crazy. But either I am crazy or the governor is.' When he asked why I thought that, I explained my difficulty about the typewriter and paper. I told him how the governor told me to write, but would not give me the paper to write on. He laughingly told me that I was certainly not crazy and told me he would see what he could do for me. After a few more visits to the shrink, and many more weekly requests to Reilly, I came in from the yard one afternoon to find the typewriter and ream of paper on my bed in my cell. It had taken a year to get it.

I continued on my case and my law studies and Tommy and I kept up our discussions on our walks in the prison yard. They became quite animated at times; his input helped me feel alive and hopeful. I continued to be asked by other prisoners to study their cases, and that helped me increase my knowledge. I began to see that in some cases an error might be made which favoured the prosecution. It might be a genuine error, and it might not. Sometimes, as far as I could see, a concerted effort was made to get a conviction, regardless of the truth. I began to look at every aspect of my case and began to discover the inconsistencies.

In 1984 I re-read George Orwell's book of the same title. He completed the book in 1948 and got its title by altering that to 1984. I first read it as a young man. I had always admired his writing and, after all, 'Big Brother' was surely watching me. So I read 1984 again and was again impressed with Orwell's vision of the future. So many of the things he forecast in his book had already come to pass.

I decided to mark the year, and his book, by making some changes in my life. I stopped smoking. The first three days were the hardest. There was a programme in my yoga book for stopping smoking and I followed that. Basically it advised deep breathing when the urge to smoke got strong, and alternative nostril breathing at night if it was difficult to sleep. It explained that the stomach pangs felt after stopping smoking were not hunger pangs but withdrawal symptoms. Deep breathing solved that too.

My first smoking experience had been when I was 7 years old. Myself and a few pals were going to the cinema for the Saturday matinée and we wanted to get cigs. Now I knew that my Dad got five Woodbines from Donoghue's shop each morning and evening. There was rationing at that time but I did not understand how all that worked, so I went in to Donoghue's and bought five woodbines and a box of matches, which Mrs Donoghue thought were for my Dad. Off we went to the pictures and we puffed our way through the five woodbines, with a lot of coughing and spluttering. Woodbines were the strongest cigs back then.

Back at home that evening having our tea, my Dmumad seemed very pleased with me. And when the meal was over he said, 'Ok son, you were very thoughtful to collect my cigs. I'll have them now.' My heart dropped, and for a second I was in a blind panic. I knew I was in trouble. But if I lied I'd be in even bigger trouble. So I told the truth, cringing as I saw the anger and disbelief in his face. I got a few good clatters – he was disgusted with me – and I was sent to bed early that evening. For days afterwards he'd be muttering to himself when he'd look at me. He wasn't a violent man and seldom slapped us. It was only later that I realised the enormity of my action. Rationing meant that cigs were very scarce, and he looked forward to his ration very much.

After a month or so without tobacco I stopped drinking coffee. I found this harder than when I stopped smoking. I got headaches and my nerves were on edge. Again I used yoga and meditation and over time that wore off and I felt better. Having gone this far I decided to become vegetarian. This was not as drastic as it may sound because the meat in the prison diet was, to say the least, unappetising. That completed my tribute to Orwell and 1984. No more nicotine, coffee or meat!

15

ventually Tommy was released. I missed his company and our discussions but I was determined to continue. Curiously enough, most prisoners have no interest in the law or the workings of the law; the Constitution might have been a far distant planet in space as far as they were concerned. I was an oddity, a headcase, spending all my time studying. As if I could possibly get my conviction overturned! They preferred to play football in the yard or pump iron in the gym.

When Dominic McGlinchey, a well-known figure in the movement, was re-extradited back into the state from the North he was returned to Portlaoise Prison. He used to come in to my cell after breakfast and we would talk, discussing his case and the law until exercise time at 10 a.m. We became friends and often walked together in the yard, much to the annoyance of some of his INLA colleagues who did not speak to me because I insisted on being my own man and not getting involved with them. Dominic and I usually walked together in the yard.

I made enquiries about the process called thin-layer chromatography. This was the process the state laboratory forensic scientist, used when he claimed that he could match a wool fibre said to have been found in a getaway car with wool fibres from the sweater I was wearing when I was arrested. I wrote to the Northern Ireland Forensic Science Laboratory and discovered that it was scientifically impossible to conclusively prove a match between wool fibres by way of Thin Layer Chromotography, as the Prosecution had purported to do at my trial. I was not surprised.

I began to look at the evidence of Professor Harbison, the Chief State Pathologist. I saw that he arrived to examine the bodies of the two dead Gardaí on the evening of 7 July 1980, but did not carry out the post-mortem until the following day. This made no sense to me, considering the situation at the time. There were two dead Gardaí and three fugitives being sought. Early ballistics reports could be very important.

I examined his trial evidence regarding the fatal entry wound which killed Garda Henry Byrne. He had been asked why he had not measured the abrasion collar of the wound, the bruised area around the actual hole. He said he did not have time to do so and also claimed that the entry wound, which measured 10mm, could not have been caused by a 9mm bullet and had be caused by a .45, .450 or .455 (11mm) bullet. The prosecution claimed that the raiders used such a revolver but no such weapon was ever recovered. In the course of my studies I found a judgement of the Court of Criminal Appeal, a court superior to the Special Criminal Court. This judgement, in the appeal of Harry White in 1947, found the reverse. It found that a 10mm entry wound could not have been caused by a .45 (11mm) bullet and was caused by a 9mm bullet. It was becoming clear to me that Harbison's evidence was open to question, to say the least.

This aroused my curiosity regarding this man. I made further enquiries and discovered that, at the time of the trial, he was a part-time lecturer in Trinity College, Dublin. I went back to his evidence and saw that he was addressed as 'Professor Harbison' and answered on oath to that title when he was actually only a part-time lecturer.

One night I was awakened about midnight by loud and prolonged cheering from the other prisoners. I got out of bed and tapped on the heating pipe to my next-door neighbour to ask what was happening. He told me that, according to the twelve o'clock news on the radio, Chief Stack had been shot dead in Dublin. Prisoners continued cheering and banging on their cell doors for quite a while, in spontaneous reaction to the demise of this much-detested prison official. It transpired that he was not yet dead but had been mortally wounded. The following morning, Governor Reilly and the other chief, John Keaveney, came into the block doing their rounds. The tension was palpable as they walked slowly on their inspection along the E1 landing. On every landing, prisoners stood at their cell doors silently watching them. They had only walked about a quarter of the way along the landing when a voice from high above, probably E4, spoke loudly and clearly, 'You're next, John.' The governor and chief turned on their heels and quickly left the landing, exiting the block. The tension burst, and everyone erupted in laughter.

Some time later, the Prison Officers' Association held its annual convention. The Portlaoise Branch proposed a motion saying that they would not condone brutality against prisoners and would not protect any officer involved in such an action. It was passed unanimously, and conditions improved noticeably after that. The security searches continued but the jailers were much less aggressive. Chief Stack died nearly a year later.

Time passed as it inevitably does. I continued with my legal work, interspersed with walks in the yard and woodwork in the workshop. I enjoyed making carvings and learned to do wood-turning. Then there was another big security scare. Explosives had been found hidden in some wood in the Provo workshop and woodworking was stopped altogether. Each political section had its own facilities. But an incident in one area had repercussions in every area.

Education in prisons became a big thing within the EU, and also in Irish prisons. The Department of Justice Coordinator of Education in Irish prisons was Kevin Warner. We prisoners in Portlaoise tended to have a sceptic's view of officials, no matter what department they worked in, and I think we did not realise, or appreciate at first, the good work done by Mr Warner. He was responsible for setting up education in Portlaoise, as well as other Irish prisons, and he did a splendid job.

Classes were set up in Portlaoise. We could study a wide variety of subjects; a yoga teacher was even brought in to give classes. Joan was a great teacher and I was delighted to get proper instruction instead of trying to learn from a book in my cell. She was very spiritual, as was her teaching of yoga. Most of the prisoners wanted the physical and not the spiritual, and so gradually her class dwindled until, after a year, I was her only student on our landing. I was truly blessed. For some eighteen months I had a one-to-one class each week with her.

About 1987, Brian Maguire came in to teach art. I went to his introductory talk without the slightest interest in painting, which was his forte; I was then only interested in trying to get the woodworking back. When Brian started I was approached by a couple of prisoners to attend his class on our landing. They needed me to make up the necessary minimum of four students to justify having a class. I agreed reluctantly and the classes commenced. When Brian had introduced himself he sat us at the big table, two each side, facing each other. He put out a palette for each of us, gave us some brushes and paper and told two of us to make a portrait of the other two. Walking out of the room, he said he would be back in half an hour. When he returned he switched us around and gave a similar instruction, and left us again for another half an hour. When he came back and pinned our efforts up on the wall he was able to tell which piece each of us had painted. It was amazing. I was hooked, and continued painting from then on.

Painting proved to be very important for me in prison. I enjoyed learning and exploring colour, tone, shape and harmony. And I went at it wholeheartedly. It took me away from studying law, and even from the prison. I remembered having read about Prince Kropotkin, the Russian anarchist, and what he said about being in prison. To paraphrase, he reckoned that each person had memories and visions and imaginings and that each of these was multi-coloured. But the colour of prison is grey. Gradually the colours of the memories, visions and imaginings of the prisoner fade in proportion to the time spent in prison. If, over time, the colours fade to the greyness of the prison then the prisoner is truly lost. I determined that this would not happen to me. Painting brought me colour and shape and harmony not otherwise open to me in the prison environment. It was also a challenge, and very satisfying to me who never before considered that I might be able to make a painting.

Brian brought Theresa McKenna and Michael O'Dea from the National College of Art and Design (NCAD) into the prison. They worked with us for a couple of years. Other artists were brought in too. But Brian, Theresa and Michael set things moving, each with their different styles, and all with serious commitment to the project. Basically, I had one class per week with one or other of them over a period of thirteen weeks. Sometimes during the college holiday period Brian would arrange for a different artist to come in and give a workshop. Once I started painting I kept at it on an almost daily basis.

Theresa was very sensitive to our needs, in our isolation from the world. She brought in various things for us to draw and paint. Sometimes she brought flowers or leaves, and sometimes fabrics. Once she brought seaweed. When I smelled it I had to excuse myself. It had such an effect on me that I went to my cell and wept, with longing for the sea. After a while I was able to return to the class and make drawings of the seaweed. Another time she brought in her little terrier. She left him with me for an hour so that I could draw him. All I could do was sit and look at him, talk to him and enjoy his company. I got very little drawing done in that session. But I had a great time.

It is always hardest for the person with someone in prison, and so it was for Eva. She continued visiting me regularly, leaving me money, books and clothes. She was very generous and supportive during most of my time in prison. She persevered for years, but then told me she was finished with me. She had found someone else and wanted to make a life for herself. While I was sorry, and quite disappointed, I understood and could see her position. I wished her all the best. In the cell on my own I had a good cry, which helped me a lot. After some weeks she wrote to me asking if she could visit me again and we continued more or less as before. About a year later she again told me she was leaving me but six weeks after that she was back and life returned to 'normal' between us again.

Being in relationship with someone in prison causes huge pain and grief for both parties. If the prisoner is serving a long sentence it is even more damaging. Relationships rarely survive in such circumstances. I remember one time a neighbour was looking very glum. I asked him what the matter was and he told me his wife was not coming to see him again as she had found someone else. He asked me what he should do.

'When you're locked up tonight, and are alone in your cell, have a good cry for yourself. It will help,' I advised.

'Are you mad?' he replied, 'I don't cry. Fuck off!'

'Look around you,' I told him. 'Do you think all these hard men are always like that? Do you think they don't have a quiet cry to themselves when they are alone in their cells?'

But he was having none of it and again told me to fuck off and stormed away down the landing. He did not speak to me again that day or the next, and I noticed him glaring at me as he passed by. But two days later as I was getting some bread for my breakfast he came up to me and said, 'Hey Peter, you were right. It worked. Thanks.' It took a minute before I realised what he was talking about.

'Did you? As I suggested the other day?' I asked.

'Yes,' he replied, 'but don't tell anybody.' Then he strolled away, smiling to himself.

Other friends visited me too. Eoin and Eva Burke came from Galway. Gerry McNern, whom I used to fish with, came from

Donegal. Christy Moore, the wonderful singer/songwriter, visited from Dublin. They all came regularly to see me. The poet Paul Durcan wrote to me and was very supportive. He sent me a copy of each of his latest books as they were published. He is a wonderful poet and it was a pleasure reading them. He would also send me a card when he was away on tour, which was very thoughtful of him and brought me something of outside events.

Clarrie and the children had great difficulty just making ends meet. And with visiting so awkward they rarely got to see me. But my eldest son Thomas, at the age of 14, decided to come on his own. His visits were very special to me. And my admiration for him grew and grew as he did. In order to visit me he had to travel from Killybegs to Donegal. From there he would take the bus to Dublin, a trip of over four hours. He would then spend the night in Dublin with his uncle Paddy and travel down to Portlaoise the following morning. And of course after the visit he had to make the return journey. All of this when he was only 14 years old. After visiting conditions had improved we could finally hug each other. At first my arms went in a downward slant, but over the years as he grew taller my arms had to reach higher and higher, until the situation was reversed with him reaching around me in a downward slant. At first I could lift him in our hugging but later he was the one who did the lifting. My youngest son John just could not face coming into the prison after that first 'welfare visit' when I was still sentenced to death. Several times he started out to come with Thomas but he was too young and it was simply too much for him. He returned home. This was not all that unusual, as several other people found it too excruciating having to face into the prison to visit. Thomas visiting me also connected me to my other children as he would bring me news of how they were, which somewhat eased the pain of separation and isolation.

As time passed, Anna and Lulu had to emigrate to the US. They lived and worked in New York and could only visit on their occasional holidays home to Ireland. I've always felt that my family suffered more than me when I was in prison. I lived my time inside but they could only imagine what it was like for me, gleaning only the limited account I was allowed to give on visits or in letters. They also had to deal with the fact of their father at first being under sentence of death and then facing forty years in prison. A prison sentence affects more than just the prisoner and can be devastating for family and friends. Being locked away for such a long time deprived me and my children of the possibility of our re-uniting. It is possible that I might have got sober. It is possible that having got sober I might have been able to reconnect with my family in a positive way. Those reasonable possibilities were denied to me, and to my family, by my being wrongfully imprisoned.

Listening to the radio one day I heard some people talking, as if with authority, about prison and being in prison. And I realised just how difficult it is to describe prison to someone who has never experienced it. Arising from this, I wrote the following:

Prison Day
Grey ...
all grey
grey shades
each day
shades ...
of grey.
Cold day
stone grey
cold stone
steel grey.
But ...
blue paint
you say

blue?
nay! ...
blue grey.
Cold steel
stone grey
wearisome ...
each day.
Dark grey
or light
each day ...
grey
et cetera
et cetera
until ...
final day
dawns grey
passing
all away ...
to clay.

Wednesday 13 August 1986

16

And so the years passed and I survived through my legal studies, yoga, meditation and my painting. Prison life was not easy. And being in a top-security prison, with all the paranoia consequent to that, could be very trying at times. Nevertheless, E Block of Portlaoise was probably the best place in the state to do time in. We did not do prison work or wear prison clothes, and insisted on being addressed by our names. The Provos had established their independence within the prison and had their own elected leaders who negotiated with the prison authorities on behalf of their members. On E1 we also elected our spokesperson who acted on our collective behalf as needs be. Group solidarity was a protection against harassment from jailers and the authorities. Sometimes there would be a split, and our landing would be divided between the two factions, at least until such time as the schism would be healed. I stayed out of these situations as I was an unaligned political prisoner.

Prison is like a microcosm of life on the outside. Simple, and sometimes silly, things could become exaggerated into major issues. This was especially true of groups or individuals who were insecure in themselves. I tried to stay clear of all such issues, and was fortunate to make friends with men of like mind who could laugh off such antics. Danny Lyons, a fellow Dubliner, and I often walked together and had some laughs. When he was only 12 years old he was locked up in an industrial school until he reached 16 years. He was severely abused and tortured while incarcerated and it almost ruined his life. Yet he was a survivor and could enjoy a laugh. We did not take ourselves too seriously, and that was an important component for staying calm and sane inside.

Brendan Hughes was another very interesting character. He was a quiet person and one could be forgiven for thinking that he was just that. But it was he who organised the famous helicopter escape of the three senior republicans from Mountjoy Prison in 1973, and he also put together the escape of nineteen republican prisoners from Portlaoise in 1974. Then circumstances left him outside the Provos, and at one stage he was being hunted by the authorities North and South as well as the Provos. Thankfully he survived and was a positive influence in Portlaoise. He had become a friend early on and we spent many hours in conversation, walking in the yard.

In 1988 an industrial dispute arose between the jailers and the state. The jailers went on strike, which lasted about six weeks, and during this time senior prison management opened and locked cells. Gardaí were on duty in the prison and the kitchen was run by the army, which was an unexpected bonus for us because we got army food, which was 100 per cent better than the prison fare we usually got. The army also played a major security role.

When I learned that the jailers had a picket outside the prison I took no visits during the dispute. As far as I was concerned I would not pass a strike picket and I would not participate in anyone else passing one. The other inmates did not see the principle involved and took their visits as usual.

When the strike ended and jailers returned to work the food deteriorated to what it had been previously and the governor refused to improve it. Then one day all the Provos threw their dinners out onto the wire mesh between the landings. The food fell through to the ground below, with some of it caught on the mesh. This was done with every successive meal until the governor agreed to improve the food. Although it never came to army food standard it was better than before, and more tolerable.

During the strike, Brendan and I were walking in the yard when we spotted a black cat in a sort of alcove between the prison block and the Provo workshop. Apparently she had been living around the staff canteen and when they went on strike she moved to our yard. We got some milk and put it on the ground near the cracked ventilation opening, under the workshop where she had disappeared. We sat quietly, and soon she came out, tentatively, and drank the milk. She accepted our presence as benign and then went back under the workshop. In a few moments she re-appeared with a tiny black kitten in her jaws. When she brought it to us we saw that its eyes were swollen and closed. I went inside and got some Optrex from my cell, which I diluted with water, and also a clean cloth. She was still there, with Brendan and her kitten, when I returned. He held the kitten and I gently bathed its eyes and washed away the pus gathered there. It opened its little eyes and mewed. And its mum carried it back under the workshop, returning immediately with another kitten in similar condition. She had four kittens altogether and brought each of them to us for treatment. We figured that she had given birth under the workshop and the wood dust had infected the kittens' eyes.

After that we brought them food regularly and she adopted me as her human. I called her Kate. When it came time for me to go walking in the yard she would be waiting as I walked around the corner of the workshop, and often perched across my shoulders as I walked up and down. It was a wonderful gift for me having her in the yard as a friend. I got a box and made her a shelter with an old sweater of mine as a blanket and she was very content. A tomcat came visiting her from time to time and she had three litters before the prison authorities began to mutter about cats. Eventually I got permission to give Kate out to Eva and some of her offspring were released to other visitors. I was glad they had good homes but I missed Kate and her extended family about the place.

Some of the men secretly made booze, called hooch, from various ingredients in plastic gallon containers. When the hooch was deemed ready for consumption a small group would gather in a cell to drink it. I have to admit that at such times, especially if it was a good batch, the smell of it, and the social occasion, tempted me sorely. Thank heavens I resisted that temptation, which was very powerful at times, and I never sampled the stuff. By that time I had realised that I was powerless over alcohol and I was obsessed with working my case towards getting my conviction quashed and my freedom restored. Still, I sometimes consoled myself with the thought that when I got out I would be able to enjoy a proper drink. Such lunacy!

A friend left me in the *Big Book of Alcoholics Anonymous*, and with his prompting I read it. Although at that time I understood little in it, I did grasp the fact that I was powerless over alcohol. Actually the visits and letters from friends who were in the Fellowship of AA helped me enormously throughout my prison years. At that time AA meetings did not exist in E Block. But my friends, the Big Book and my obsession with my case kept me sober. I know now that my Higher Power was watching over me, although I would have scoffed at such a notion back then.

Portlaoise is a very old, Victorian prison. Each cell has an air vent which is tiny on the inside with a larger metal grille on the outside wall. The outside grille to my cell had some bars missing, which allowed starlings to nest inside the opening. When the chicks were born I could hear them chirping for food as the parents came to feed them. I so enjoyed watching the parents as they flew away for food and back again in relays. They did this non-stop from dawn to dusk. Sometimes one would land on my windowsill, waiting for their partner to finish the feeding. I began to put out little pieces of cheese, which they loved. The hen was the most trusting and she would come to my window calling for food if I had neglected to put some out.

She came back to that nesting place for three years and I looked forward very much to her return each year. She would come into my cell and take food from my hand. It was funny watching her when she returned to feed her chicks with worms held in her beak, as she also tried to pick up bits of cheese. Her beak looked like a kebab, with all the bits on it. Starlings have a lifespan of about five years and I was honoured that she had shared so much of her life with me.

Word got out around the landing about my starling friends and unfortunately not everyone approved. One sick individual caught a starling on his windowsill by putting a snare out with food in the middle. He then plucked the poor bird alive and boasted to his buddies about it. When I was told about it I was furious and could not eat my dinner that day. But as I thought about it in my cell I realised he was trying to get at me. He and his friends probably expected me to go for him, which could also be a larger snare. When I got out of my cell, two prisoners came to me to talk about what had happened, offering their support if I wanted to deal with the individual. I said, 'Only a coward would do what he did, and only a sick coward would boast about it. And only sick cowards would support him and what he did. I would not dirty my hands on the likes of him. He is below contempt.' And with that I went for a walk in the yard. My response was of course relayed back to him. And he had very few friends afterwards, and I never heard that he plucked another bird.

During one winter the heating system broke down. For about six weeks there was no heat at all in our E Block. It was freezing cold, with the dampness running down the cell walls. Everything in the cell was damp. I used to put my underwear between the blankets at night, for two reasons: to help me get warm and to keep them from becoming damp. I heard that on the top floor, E4, icicles were hanging from the ceilings of some of the cells. I had previously hurt my back while working in the meat factory in Kildare. During that cold spell I got sciatica, a very painful condition. I went to the doctor, who after a long time asked for a specialist to visit the prison. This specialist put me on a course of tablets for a month to relax the sciatic nerve. He told me they might heal it but if not I would have to be on painkillers for the rest of my life. I took the tablets as instructed and got relief for about three months. But then the condition got worse.

Determined not to go on painkillers I decided to apply my practices of meditation and yoga to my sciatica. At first I could barely move. It took me a long time to dress and especially to tie my shoelaces; even getting out of bed was a torture. On one occasion the jailers came in to search my cell before opening time and I was ordered out of bed. When I explained that because of my back I could hardly move I was simply dragged from the bed on to the floor. They did not stand on ceremony.

I began doing the yoga practice called Salute to the Sun every morning. At first I could not even raise my hands fully above my head, but I persevered, because in truth I had no other option. Gradually, through meditation and yoga, my condition improved, and after seven months I was clear of it. I knew that I needed to be careful for a while, especially not to get draughts on my back which could exacerbate the condition. I asked the doctor for a heater and a chair in my cell due to my bad back and was allowed them. This was real luxury! On cold mornings there was often a gathering of neighbours for tea and yarns around the heater.

Although it was possible to make friends in prison, such friendships seldom continued after release. Sometimes before a person was due for release he would ask if there was anything he could do to help me from the outside. These were generally empty offers, although well intentioned when offered. Thankfully there were exceptions. I became friends with Éamon Deegan, who was in for a couple of years, and we had many laughs together while he was in there. Before he left he told me he would help me when he got out. He was more than true to his word, organising the 'Peter Pringle Defence Committee', with such great people as Jim Brady, Brian Judge, Maurice Blythe and Joe Kelly to name but a few. As an ex-prisoner, Éamon could not visit me. But the other members did – Jim and his partner Betty McGrann, Brian and his wife Gretta. Having such support outside was a huge boost to my morale and gave me great hope for the future.

Dick Timmons, a veteran republican, had been arrested and sentenced to Portlaoise Prison and was put on our landing. He and I spent a lot of time walking in the yard and talking. He was very interesting, especially regarding the movement from the 1930s to the present. He had been imprisoned in England during the war but had escaped, making his way home to Ireland by stowing away aboard a ship from Liverpool. He was a determined little man and walked every day until he became ill. He got cancer, and there was very little medical treatment for it in the prison. They took him out to the hospital for tests but nothing much else. Myself and some other prisoners nursed him and looked after him as best we could. One jailer, T, also took an interest in Dick and helped him as much as he could; T was a decent and compassionate man. Eventually Dick got early release and died about six months later. I wrote to his wife:

Dear Mrs Timmons,

News has filtered in that Dick is dead. That is sad news indeed, and so belatedly I am writing to offer you my sincere condolences.

I knew of Dick, but I only met him for the first time when he came into this place. I had the good fortune to have him as a neighbour, so to speak. I walked and talked with him in the prison yard many, many times, and listened too, I may add, and was glad.

His illness was very sad and I hoped that following his release he might recover, but that was not to be.

I am thankful that I knew Dick; he was a good person and he brightened my existence for a while. I am sure your sorrow is great but perhaps your knowing that even in here Dick had some light-hearted times, helped others and was helped, and left behind some people who care, as I do, might be some small comfort to you and to your family. With heartfelt sympathy,

Yours sincerely,
Peter Pringle

There was a lot of bitterness on the landing about how Dick had been treated. But at least he died at home with his family and not in a prison cell. It was very important to stay healthy in prison. Some time later his daughter Claire wrote to me and came to visit. I was able to tell her how it had been for her father inside. She continued to visit me and we became good friends and she and her family were very supportive.

Dominic McGlinchey told me about Pádraigín Drinan, a solicitor in Belfast who had successfully taken a number of cases to the European Court of Human Rights. I wrote to her simply seeking guidelines in the event that I would need to go that route. She replied and came to visit me. When she realised my situation she was most helpful to me. At her suggestion I wrote to CAJ, the Committee for the Administration of Justice, in Belfast and they were supportive. She also told me about British Irish Rights Watch, a human rights group based in London headed by Michael Mansfield and Helena Kennedy, two eminent QCs. Jane Winters, the secretary and administrator of the group, became my liaison. Sister Sarah Clarke wrote to me and she was terrific, as she was for all Irish prisoners in Britain. The first newspaper to write about my case was the Andersonstown News in Belfast. And I think that came as a result of Pádraigín's support.

Reading through a law book I spotted a brief reference to the Capital Punishment Amendment Act, 1868. I got a copy of the Act, which provided for the carrying out of executions of persons convicted on indictment for 'murder'. It had never been amended to provide for execution of persons convicted on indictment for 'capital murder'. The Special Criminal Court sentenced me 'to suffer death by execution in the manner prescribed by law' for the offence of capital murder. Therefore, on my reading of the law, this was done when there was no manner prescribed by law for such execution. Here was yet another compelling reason why my trial, conviction, sentence of death and commutation to forty years' penal servitude without remission were unlawful. My rights as guaranteed under the Irish Constitution had been denied to me

In 1990 I wrote to Séamus Egan, my former senior counsel and by then a High Court judge, and told him of my findings about my case. One Sunday he came to visit me. Normally there were no visits on Sundays but High Court judges have access to prisons at any time. They even supplied an armchair for him in the visiting box. I showed him my findings, in some eight different areas of my case, including that of the chief state pathologist Dr John Harbison. I pointed out some of the flaws I had detected in Harbison's evidence, particularly in respect of what might have been seen as 'minor details'.

'It happens all the time,' he said. 'For example, suppose I am a witness in a trial and I am asked my age. And I say that I am 65 years old when I am actually 66. What difference does that make?'

'If you cannot tell the truth under oath about your age,' I replied, 'how can the court believe anything you say?'

'It happens all the time.'

'If that is so, why do you as a judge bother to officiate over the oath being administered? It seems to me that the whole procedure is a farce and the administration of justice is a sham.'

This agitated him and he arose from his chair saying, 'No, no, you are just making too much of it. And anyway, there is no way for you to get your case heard in court as the appeal process is concluded.'

'What about *habeas corpus*?' I asked him. 'Will you now hear my application for *habeas corpus*, as you are obliged to do as a judge of the High Court?'

'No,' he replied, 'I cannot. Listen, I am very sorry about your situation. The forty years' sentence is a political sentence. And you will not have to serve anything like that. I would say you'll be out in a few years.' With that he headed out the door saying, 'I'll pray for you, Peter.'

I sat there a few minutes, devastated, bound up between a huge anger, frustration and sadness. The jailer came in. I was taken to be strip-searched again, and then back to my cell.

I was in the dumps for weeks afterwards. I knew that Séamus Egan was a decent, honourable man, and I just could not square how he had responded to my revelations about my case with that decency and his status as a High Court judge. I focused on my meditation, yoga and painting. Eventually, coming out of the doldrums, I realised that if Judge Egan's attitude reflected that of the High Court I would have no chance with my case without first bringing it into the public domain.

At that time the media were not in the least interested in the Pringle Case and Eva reckoned that no one outside cared. I believed that people are inherently good and it was not a case of them not caring but of them not knowing. As far as the general public was concerned I was guilty. Because that is what the media had told them. 'It said so in the papers and on TV, so it must be true.'

In Portlaoise Prison we did not have to pay for postage except for Christmas cards. So I quietly set about spreading word of my case throughout Ireland. I wrote to the general secretaries of fifty-one trade unions, all the trade councils, the chairperson of every local authority, every government minister and every member of the Dáil and Senate. I wrote to Dr Daly the Bishop of Derry, who replied telling me that with all the injustice in his own area he could not devote time to my case. He suggested I make contact with all of his colleagues in the South, so I wrote to every bishop of the Catholic Church and to the head of every other Church in Ireland. In the main I received very positive responses. And knowing that the Irish are great talkers I figured that word of my case would leak into the public awareness and the media would become interested. I put out about 600 letters in a year. And then I decided it was time to open my case in the High Court.

17

In January 1992 I opened my case in the High Court in Dublin by issuing a plenary summons and statement of claim in the case of Pringle v Ireland and the Attorney General. This was a civil action under the Irish Constitution. I claimed breaches of my rights under the Constitution and the failure of the state to protect my constitutional rights as it was obliged to do. I conducted my case on my own behalf. Each time I was due in court I was brought up to the Four Courts in Dublin in an elaborate escort. On the outskirts of Dublin we were met by Garda motorcycle riders who cleared traffic before us and buzzed around us as we sped into the city towards the court – all of this with the usual cacophony of loud sirens blaring.

On arrival I was taken to a holding cell on the top floor to wait until it was time for court. Then I was escorted, surrounded by jailers and Gardaí, down stairs and along corridors to the courtroom, which was always searched beforehand. My escort and I were the first people allowed to enter, and everyone entering after us was searched. I'd sit at the top bench, where senior counsel sat. Consequently, when the state SC entered he would not sit on the same bench and would sit on the bench behind, where junior barristers normally sat. They in turn sat behind their SC in the public seating. When the judge entered and the case was called by his registrar, counsel for the state stood and began to describe the case to the judge. I stood up immediately and said, 'Excuse me, what about fair play? I am the plaintiff in this case. I believe the proper procedure is for the plaintiff to open the case to the court and for the defendant to respond, not the way this is being done.' Judge Lardner, who was sitting at that time, turned to the counsel for the state saying, 'Humm, humm, yes, quite so ... Sit down, please. Well, Mr Pringle?', at which point I held my shackled arm aloft and asked for the cuffs to be removed so I could proceed. The judge agreed. And when they were removed I opened my case.

I was brought up to court several times. Kevin Haugh, SC acted for the state on a number of occasions. I found him to be courteous and open to speaking with me, which was unusual but very welcome. In July 1992 I put a motion for discovery of all state documents in my case. On that occasion Pádraic Leahy, BL was acting for the state and he tried to rubbish my motion. He said that I was only fishing to see if I could find something in my favour and that I really had no case to substantiate my claims. This was before Judge Blaney, who then asked me what I had to say. I turned to the jailer beside me and asked him to hand me a particular file from a banana box sitting on the floor beside him, which was my briefcase. Opening the file I removed three identical folders. I opened the top one and said to the court, 'I have here a sworn affidavit of one of the prosecution witnesses in my trial. He swears on oath that the statement attributed to him in the Book of Evidence was not made by him, that it is a false statement. And that furthermore he was never even asked to make a statement. I am prepared to give evidence on oath before this court that if this witness had been asked to make a statement his true statement would have meant that I could not have been convicted of crimes that I did not commit.' I offered copies of the affidavit to the court and to counsel for the state but both declined to take them.

Judge Blaney then said he would make an order for discovery in my favour, and counsel for the state asked for six months to facilitate locating all the documents, etc. I argued that it had only taken the state six weeks to put together its flawed case against me; it should not take longer to gather up the documents. The judge agreed that six months was too long and ordered that discovery be made to me, in Portlaoise Prison, within ten weeks. The state did not obey the order of the court for delivery of discovery. Each time the deadline of the court arrived without discovery having been delivered I would have another motion ready and served. Every few weeks I would appear before Judge Lardner and he would say, 'What is it now, Mr Pringle?' and I would put my motion for judgement in default, accusing the state of contempt of court. They would apologise and he would grant them yet another extension. I argued that this was wrong, and unfair to me; that if the situation was reversed and I had failed to obey the court's order he would quickly find me in contempt.

I was struggling for my life and liberty and I was not afraid to speak up when I knew I was correct. I had no time for all the bowing and scraping of lawyers before the judge. My attitude was that if I got justice I would win my case and my liberty. If not, then I would not go down without making my case as forcefully as I needed to. At such hearings the court would be filled with lawyers. I later learned they were all there to hear me, as I stood up to the state and to the judge in a way they could not. On one occasion I had the temerity to disagree with the judge and as I argued my corner I heard a whisper behind me. 'Who is he? Whoever he is, he is not afraid of his Lordship!'

Each time I appeared in court I noticed a slim, silver-haired man, dressed impeccably, who stood back and always gave me a big smile. I learned later that this was Billy, a Dubliner from the inner city who spoke in slang. He was funny and fearless. Sometimes in court when I would be having a difficult time with the judge his voice would come from the back of the court, 'You tell him, Peter!' Or else to the judge, 'Come on. Give him a break!' Or in a loud, firm Dublin accent, 'What about some justice for Peter?' It was so funny, and I very much enjoyed his comments and support. In the midst of court pomp, state power and serious opposition to my cause there was this lone voice speaking out for me, strong and fearless and proud. It lifted my heart and my morale. And it diluted all the pomp and ceremony that the system loves, and thrives on, to the subjugation of ordinary folk. I loved to see him there.

Billy wrote as he spoke, in slang, or 'ben lang' as he would say. Sometimes it would take me hours to decipher his language. He even wrote to Revd Dr Ian Paisley, MP in Westminster, seeking his assistance in my case. In his letter, which he sent by registered post, he told Dr Paisley that his reputation would be ruined if it got out that Billy had written to him. Paisley's secretary wrote back to Billy telling him that as I was outside Dr Paisley's jurisdiction there was nothing he could do. Billy wrote to the reverend again, complaining that the least he would have expected from him was that he'd 'sign his old letter himself' and not get a secretary to do so. Billy was great.

The superior courts have very long holidays, and the summer break is from the end of July until almost mid-October. This non-productive period was quite demoralising for me in prison, just waiting and waiting. In October 1992 I saw a small article in the *Guardian* newspaper. It told of how a woman named Sonia Jacobs, who had been on death row and a long time in prison in Florida, had her convictions overturned and regained her freedom. This impressed me very much. And I thought that if this woman could do it in the US then maybe I could do it here. That article really lifted my morale just when I needed it.

Eventually, in January 1993, I received a pile of documents with a sworn affidavit from the Chief State Solicitor's Office that this comprised full discovery – although I later found out this was not true. At the time it was very interesting, and even exciting, for me to examine the state documents. I found a photocopy of a crucial notebook belonging to the detectives who swore on oath, during my trial, that he had recorded the interrogations in this notebook. He had claimed that I had said the words upon which I was convicted and sentenced to death. Those words were, 'I know that you know

I was involved but on the advice of my solicitor I am saying nothing and you will have to prove it all the way.' He claimed that he had entered them in his notebook when I said them during a particular interrogation. Examination of his notebook, however, records me as saying those words at 9.28 a.m., yet this entry in the notebook appears before the entry recording his interrogation of me starting at 8.25 a.m. that same day. And furthermore, those words could not have been an accurate record of my interrogation, because I never said them.

The discovery documents also revealed that my photo had been shown to a number of prosecution witnesses, after my arrest and before the trial. When Garda Boyle identified the man in the public gallery as the man he had tried to arrest, prosecuting counsel told the court he had been shown my photo before the trial. It was not revealed to the trial court that other prosecution witnesses had also been shown my photo.

I received a copy of the Garda Investigation Report, which was sent to the Director of Public Prosecutions (DPP) resulting in his decision to prosecute me. Had that report been true and accurate I doubt if I would have been prosecuted.

I also found a document that had been circulated by the then Assistant Commissioner, John Paul McMahon, to every member of the Gardaí two days before my arrest. The document instructed that Peter Pringle should be arrested and detained under Section 30 of the Offences Against the state Act, 1939, for the murder of a Garda. This document stated that I was dangerous and that I was addicted to alcohol and drugs. While I was definitely addicted to alcohol I was not addicted to drugs, which were not my thing at all.

Séamus Egan, my former SC, had been elevated from the High Court to the Supreme Court, and I wrote telling him of some of the new facts I had uncovered in my case. He wrote back in his own hand, on his own Supreme Court headed notepaper. He opened his letter, written on 2 November 1993:

Dear Peter,

Thanks for your letter. I feel very sorry for you as, in my view, the evidence was not sufficient to convict you of murder.

Coming from a serving Supreme Court Judge this was a powerful opinion on my case. It was without precedent. I sent the letter out to my defence committee for safe keeping. They showed it to Maeve Sheehan, then a young journalist with the Sunday Tribune.

The state entered a motion to have my case struck out. The hearing was conducted before Judge Murphy, and in his judgement, delivered on 19 November 1993, he ruled that most of my case was 'an abuse of process'. This was based upon the finality of decisions of the Court of Criminal Appeal. In effect he ruled out anything relating to the trial court and the appeal court. He did not, however, rule out my claims in relation to my death sentence. In the course of his judgement he said:

If the contentions of the plaintiff are correct, not only were the criminal proceedings flawed but they were flawed with the result that an innocent man was convicted of the most serious crimes and deprived of his liberty and nearly forfeited his very life.

He ended his judgement as follows:

Finally, I would like to add that I believe that the issue and motion before me raise dramatically a matter which is of great public importance. It is for that reason I would welcome an appeal to the Supreme Court and in that event I would be anxious that the Legal Aid Board would be informed that it is my view that whatever legal assistance is required should be available to Mr Pringle if he seeks it.

Shortly after that judgement was delivered I had a visit from an elderly solicitor whom I did not know. A senior partner in a large respected law firm based in Dublin, he told me he had been following my case with interest. He said I was doing very well and had brought my case further than many a lawyer could in such a short time. But he also told me to be wary and to consider engaging a legal team because, he said, judges do not like giving big decisions to lay litigants. He said it was always much easier for them to give such decisions 'within the club' to lawyers and in a non-personal sense.

Alone in my cell at night I found it hard to keep my optimism alive, especially when the courts were on holidays. I did my yoga and my meditation and some light reading. One day, browsing in the library, I saw a title which caught my eye, *When the Sacred Ginmill Closes*, a thriller by Lawrence Block. I had not read Block before, but enjoyed his writing immediately. This particular novel dealt with the principal character finding sobriety and it really resonated with me. It was exactly what I needed to read at the time.

Maeve Sheehan came to visit me and asked my permission to print the letter from Judge Egan as part of an article she wanted to write on my situation. Although I was very glad she wanted to publish the article, I would not allow her to include Judge Egan's letter. I felt that it would not be right for me to do that. She tried to persuade me, telling me it was a powerful testament and could be very helpful to me. I knew that, but I could not bring myself to agree to allow her publish his letter. She accepted my decision but persisted, contacting Judge Egan as part of her investigation.

Judge Egan gave Maeve permission to publish his letter to me. She wrote a long article featuring the letter and this appeared on the front page of the *Sunday Tribune* on 19 December 1993. It caused quite a stir, and other newspapers followed up on it.

Audrey Magee of the *Irish Times* also visited me. Her article, with photos of Judge Egan and of me, as well as part of his letter, appeared on 30 December 1993. The first article by Maeve followed by Audrey's gave potency to my case in the eyes of the public, and even the judiciary. And it was noticeable to me that I was treated with respect when I went to court after that.

Among the cards I received that Christmas was one from Greg O'Neill, a human rights solicitor in Dublin, and his staff, wishing me well. He offered me his assistance. Then at the end of December new legislation called the Criminal Procedure Act, 1993, came into law. This new law, in effect, extended the criminal process, which up to then started on arrest and ended at the final appeal. This new law provided that where new facts were uncovered that might reveal a miscarriage of justice a sentenced person could go back to the Court of Criminal Appeal and get a new appeal.

In January 1994 I got permission to phone Greg O'Neill. He came to visit me and I gladly took up his offer of assistance. He retained Barry White, SC and Anthony Salmon, BL and we worked on preparation of the case to go before the Court of Criminal Appeal under the new legislation, which they reckoned was the best way forward.

In accordance with Judge Murphy's ruling and suggestion I had already served notice of appeal against his decision to the Supreme Court. Appearing before that court in January 1994 I again represented myself. In the course of that hearing I told the court that Greg O'Neill was coming into my case and that we would likely go before the Court of Criminal Appeal under the new legislation. This seemed to please the court. I was given leave to follow that path and to re-enter my appeal to the Supreme Court at my discretion.

We needed to raise funds in order to retain various experts to examine the state's reports and findings therein. My defence committee began to raise money by organising various functions, like race nights, music sessions, etc. Billy wrote to me and sent money he collected from youngsters in his neighbourhood. One day I got a letter from a Martin Cahill telling me his friends had organised a session in a pub and had collected over £900 for my defence, which he sent to me in postal orders. When I showed the letter to Dominic

McGlinchey he laughed and said to me, 'Do you know who this is?' And when I told him I hadn't a clue he said, 'That's "the General", Martin Cahill is "the General".' Then it sank in, and I was amazed that someone I did not know, and who according to the media was a notorious criminal, would bother about me and my situation. But I was very grateful. And it goes to show that one should treat media reports with discretion.

The committee raised enough money to allow Greg to retain the necessary experts from Britain. I had put together a comprehensive case covering almost every aspect of the state's case against me. Some of these were legal arguments, or what is sometimes termed by the media as 'technicalities'. My lawyers explained that courts tended to address just one point and would not address any other if that one point was deemed to be sufficient. My feeling was, and is, that such attitude does not do justice to a case; each point put to a court should be properly addressed by it. But after trying to argue my views on the matter I felt I had little option but to go their way.

In any event, they prepared a case for me to go before the Court of Criminal Appeal, and in autumn 1994 it was opened before that court. Presiding was Judge O'Flaherty of the Supreme Court and Judges Morris and Lavin of the High Court sat with him.

My case opened. And while it was ongoing Greg went with one of our experts to the state laboratory during a lunch break. They arrived unannounced into the office, and found files with my name on one of them! Greg returned to court with a sworn affidavit, and when the court learned that full discovery had not been made the court made a further order for discovery and adjourned the hearing until April 1995.

When the state handed over this further discovery it contained some 600 additional pages of material. This was not insignificant and required considerable study by my lawyers and myself. They claimed, again, in a sworn affidavit that this was full discovery, which we found out later was, again, not the truth.

he IRA cessation of hostilities in the North and the possibility of peace created considerable speculation. We had already heard on the grapevine that dialogue had been established between republican and loyalist prisoners in the North, and this gave impetus towards a future peace process. I was not privy to the Provo debate and discussions within the prison but I gathered that, with an end to the war and an emerging process towards peace, there would be an amnesty for the prisoners. The prospect of early release caused much excitement within the prison.

My case reopened in April 1995. Almost every day during the hearings Rex Mackey, SC, one of the most senior lawyers practising at that time and highly respected, came into the court and stood to one side, near me. He greeted me silently and nodded to me when he was leaving, to indicate his support for my position. On one occasion, as I was being escorted along the corridor to the lift on the way to the holding cell on the top floor, a senior Garda walking alongside me asked me what I was looking for in my case. When I said I wanted my conviction quashed he said, 'Are you claiming you're innocent?'

'I am innocent,' I replied.

'You mean you were framed?'

'Yes.'

'But why would our fellas frame you?'

'I don't know for sure, but maybe because I am a republican. I was interned in The Curragh in the '50s.'

'Oh,' he said, 'that would be enough reason alright. I understand now.'

And the conversation ended as we entered the lift. The next time I met him, and as he was escorting me again, he asked, 'Why didn't you sort this out when you were detained in the Garda station?'

'Well I had a drink problem,' I told him, 'and when I was arrested I was in the jigs at the end of a long binge. I wasn't in a fit state to deal with it at all.'

'Oh,' he said, 'I understand. So that's how it happened.'

And I somehow knew that he did understand, although I didn't know how until much later.

A key element of our case was the circumstances surrounding the handling of a sample of my blood taken by a Detective Sergeant when my nose was bleeding during my detention in the Garda barracks. He had given a number of different accounts of this matter. We had his documents, showing those contradictions. In the copy of his notebook supplied to me in discovery he recorded that my nose was bleeding. But he did not mention this fact in his statement of evidence for my trial, nor did he mention it in his sworn evidence during my trial.

When he was called into evidence in 1995 he concocted a totally different, and previously unheard, version of events surrounding the blood sample. He cited another Garda officer, who was present in court, as his witness. But when that officer was called into evidence he refuted the first officer's version of events, stating it had never happened. Another Garda officer, who was assisting the second officer at the relevant time, also refuted the version of events of the first witness in his sworn testimony.

Greg had retained a documents expert from England to examine the state's forensics report. This expert was called into evidence and stated that upon examination of the report he had found one part which had been tippexed over. Counsel for the state asked him what had been underneath the tippexed part but my expert said that he could not tell because the document he had examined was only a photocopy.

'Why did you not examine the original?'

'I understand it is not available,' replied my expert.

'Don't you know it is in the Chief State Solicitor's Office?' counsel for the state responded.

With that, my Senior Counsel said that this was the first our side had heard of it, and the court broke for lunch to allow our expert time to examine the original. So much for the earlier claim of full discovery!

When the afternoon session began our expert was called and gave evidence of his examination of the original report and his findings. He reported that a sentence in the report had been tippexed over to change its meaning and make it look as though certain evidence against me was conclusive when it wasn't. This was a shocking discovery, which was even obvious from the faces of the judges. The state forensic scientist was called into evidence. He acknowledged that the report was his and that he had made the change in the report. Yet he swore that he could not remember why he had done this.

When our case was completed and the state's efforts at rebuttals ended, Judge O'Flaherty declared that judgement was reserved. Counsel for the state asked that if the court decided to quash my convictions it should order a retrial.

I was returned to Portlaoise Prison to await the verdict. On 16 May 1995 I was brought back to the court and Judge O'Flaherty read it out. He went through the issues in the case, but not all of them. The court quashed my convictions as being 'unsafe and unsatisfactory' and then ordered a retrial. It is an amazing judgement for its inconsistencies. The court had a number of documents before it, showing a crucial Garda witness giving different accounts of events. The Appeal Court heard that the detective gave a previously unheard version, which was rebutted by two of his colleagues, all on oath. But the court did not find that any Garda officer had lied. In its judgement it found that, 'It would, in the court's view, be wholly unreasonable to expect witnesses to retain over a period of approximately fourteen years a clear and unambiguous recollection of events.'

The same judgement ordered my retrial by the Special Criminal Court, knowing that if a witness could not be expected to remember accurately what happened in 1980 his evidence at any retrial was useless and not even the Special Criminal Court could convict me on that basis. When the judgement had been read out, Barry White rose and asked the court to hear a bail application. Judge Morris told Barry that he would be presiding over the Special Criminal Court the following day and would hear a bail application at 2 p.m.

I was taken back to prison and the following day brought before the Special Criminal Court presided over by Judge Morris for my bail application, which was vigorously opposed by the state. I was called into evidence. Barry asked if I had applied for bail before my trial in 1980. I said I had and that it was refused. Judge Morris asked me if that was before this court. And I said it was. It was then stated that I had not applied for bail to the High Court, to which I replied, 'That is not so. I applied for bail to the High Court and was refused there also.' All three members of the court sat up straighter, looked at each other and then focused intently on me.

'Are you telling the court that you applied to the High Court for bail and were refused?' Judge Morris asked me.

'That is correct,' I replied. 'If I had been granted bail then I would have been able to prepare for the trial and might not have been convicted.'

'Would you appear here for your retrial if you were granted bail today?'

'Of course I would,' I replied. 'If the state is foolish enough to continue this farce I am prepared to prove my innocence again before this or any other court.'

State counsel stood and blustered about the seriousness of capital murder, the danger of me absconding, etc. but the court ordered him to desist. It then ordered my bail, set at £50,000 and on condition that I report daily to the Gardaí. When Judge Morris turned to me, still in the witness box, I said, 'While I will be living in Galway, I will need to travel to Dublin to consult with my solicitor in preparation for the retrial.' The court then ruled that I report to the Gardaí in Galway when I was there, and in Pearse Street Garda Station when I was in Dublin. When the question of the £50,000 bail bond was raised Brian Judge went into evidence and offered to stand bail for me and to put up his home as collateral. State counsel asked him if it was the family home and then objected upon the basis that the family home could not be collateral without the consent of Brian's wife. Gretta went into evidence and gave her full consent. I was granted bail on the spot. Judge Morris told me I was free to go. When I appeared the following week, the DPP entered a *Nolle Prosequi* in my case, meaning the state was not going to proceed with a re-trial. And I was free.

I was welcomed and hugged by my son Tom and his partner Caroline, a whole group of friends and my legal team – Greg, Barry and Tony. As we were enjoying that few moments I could not help noticing the angry glares from the scowling detectives present. I also saw the senior Garda who had spoken to me in the High Court, standing in plain clothes with a big grin on his face. I approached him and said, 'I thought you were assigned to the Four Courts?'

'I am,' he replied, 'but I came here to see how you got on.'

As he shook my hand I felt the small piece of paper in his palm. I got the message and palmed it, as he said softly to me, 'Call me if you need help.'

When I looked at it later I found he had given me his name and phone number. That was an extraordinary act in the circumstances.

Surrounded by family, lawyers and friends I headed for the exit. And in that excellent company I stepped out of the court to freedom.

19

As I walked out to the sunshine I was surprised and a little intimidated by the array of press and cameras waiting outside the court. It was weird stepping from the court straight into this onslaught of questions and cameras, even though they were all friendly and encouraging. Claire, the daughter of my old friend Dick Timmons, borrowed a mobile phone from one of the journalists. She dialled a number, handed me the phone and I was able to talk to Eva, who was in Germany for a family funeral. It was amazing, standing outside the court using a telephone! That was my first use of a mobile phone, and it seemed like magic to me.

The next few hours passed in a sort of euphoric haze. Greg and I went to the RTÉ studio in Donnybrook and were interviewed on the six o'clock news. From there we went to The Barge, a large public house at Charlemont Bridge, where the party had already started. My defence committee had booked one entire floor and when Greg and I arrived we got a big cheer and lots of hugs and kisses.

The celebrations went on until closing time. I didn't drink. But everyone else got merry to say the least. At one stage a journalist arrived and asked me which one was the man just released from prison. When I told him that was me, he was surprised. 'But you are the only one sober! I thought I'd find you well on by now.'

We had a short interview and then I excused myself to rejoin my family and fiends. I did not drink when I got out because a few of the guys in the prison had warned me to be very careful that some Garda would not fit me up for something, just to get back at me. Maybe I was paranoid, but better to be safe than sorry.

It was a wonderful evening for everyone, but especially for me. I was free and with Tom and Caroline, and my defence committee friends – Éamon, Jim, Betty, Brian, Gretta, Maurice, Joe, Claire, Greg, Barry, Tony – and so many other smiling, laughing, celebrating people; I cannot remember them all by name. I was particularly glad that Billy, my supporter from the High Court, was there too. Amidst all the good cheer I felt quietly contented and happy.

I stayed with Brian and Gretta that night and I slept like a baby. In the morning I was the first awake in the house. Washed and dressed, I went downstairs to the kitchen and wandered out to their large back garden, simply enjoying the sense of it all. There was an old apple tree near the shed at the far end of the garden and on impulse I put my arms around it. Suddenly I was crying, sobbing my heart out, even as I was comforted by the beautiful old apple tree. This old tree, which regardless of injustice or ambition or greed of man, simply grew and existed in perfect harmony with the rest of nature, producing its rich fruit each year. After a while I was at peace within myself. I sat in meditation under the tree before returning to the house for some breakfast with my friends.

The days passed in a whirl. There were TV, radio and press interviews. When I was out in the streets people would call out to me, congratulating me on my release. Taxi drivers would stop and offer me a lift. It was extraordinary, and again demonstrated the good nature of people in Dublin.

When Eva returned we tried living together but it didn't work out. I blamed myself and felt that this was another thing prison had done to me. I found AA, and with it some peace within myself. I moved back to Galway and adopted a black Labrador pup who became my constant companion. We walked the hills and swam in the sea together almost every day. And I began to paint again.

I visited my children and grandchildren whenever I had the money. I moved into a house with a garden, planted some flowers and began to heal. I had the occasional relationship, but nothing lasting. And then one day I got a phone call from an American woman, Sunny Jacobs, who invited me to a talk she was giving about the death penalty. I went to hear her speak and it turned out that she was the same woman I had read about in the *Guardian* in 1992. She had also been wrongly convicted and sentenced to death, in America, and won her case. The universe had brought us together.

We now live happily together by the sea in Connemara, in sight of the hills I so loved as a youth. We have travelled the world speaking out for human rights, an end to the death penalty, and giving people hope. And we spend our days taking care of our garden, our animals and each other. We share our dream, and in that way it never ends.

Postscript

At the time of going to print, Pat McCann and Colm O'Shea remain in prison.

The man at the back of the courtroom has not been seen again.